The Transformative Potential of Participatory Budgeting

In this book, George Robert Bateman, Jr. presents a philosophical examination of the potential benefits of participatory budgeting (PB), with recommendations of how they might be realized.

The work of social philosophers like Thomas Jefferson, John Dewey, Robert Putnam are studied to better understand the potential benefits and their effect on individuals and communities. Using social provisioning and John Fagg Foster's theories of instrumental value and institutional adjustment, Bateman demonstrates how participatory budgeting in New York City (PBNYC) can realize its full potential and transform individual participants into their better selves and also transform their communities. This transformation can occur when participants are able to make decisions about things that matter in their lives. As more of us become empowered and actively engaged in deliberations concerning local economic/political issues the more we will experience public happiness, greater understanding of others, greater development of our morality, and an increased sense of belonging.

The Transformative Potential of Participatory Budgeting will be of great interest to scholars in the fields of normative political theory, political philosophy, local politics, heterodox economics, institutional economics, political sociology, urban sociology, and community sociology.

George Robert Bateman, Jr. earned his Ph.D. in Economics at the University of Missouri, Kansas City (UMKC) in 2018 through an interdisciplinary program with economics as his primary discipline and political science as his co-discipline.

Routledge Research in Public Administration and Public Policy

Contextualizing Compliance in the Public Sector
Individual Motivations, Social Processes, and Institutional Design
Saba Siddiki, Salvador Espinosa, and Tanya Heikkila

The Politics of Fracking
Regulatory Policy and Local Community Responses to Environmental Concerns
Sarmistha R. Majumdar

The Data Economy
Implications from Singapore
Sree Kumar, Warren B. Chik, See-Kiong Ng and Sin Gee Teo

Corruption Prevention and Governance in Hong Kong
Ian Scott and Ting Gong

Judicializing the Administrative State
The Rise of the Independent Regulatory Commissions in the United States,
1883–1937
Hiroshi Okayama

State Politics and the Affordable Care Act
Choices and Decisions
*Edited by John Charles Morris, Martin K. Mayer, II, Robert C. Kenter and
Luisa M. Lucero*

The Transformative Potential of Participatory Budgeting
Creating an Ideal Democracy
George Robert Bateman, Jr.

For more information about this series, please visit: www.routledge.com/
Routledge-Research-in-Public-Administration-and-Public-Policy/book-series/
RRPAPP

The Transformative Potential of Participatory Budgeting
Creating an Ideal Democracy

George Robert Bateman, Jr.

NEW YORK AND LONDON

First published 2020
by Routledge
52 Vanderbilt Avenue, New York, NY 10017

and by Routledge
2 Park Square, Milton Park, Abingdon, Oxon, OX14 4RN

Routledge is an imprint of the Taylor & Francis Group, an informa business

First issued in paperback 2021

© 2020 Taylor & Francis

The right of George Robert Bateman, Jr. to be identified as author of this work has been asserted by him in accordance with sections 77 and 78 of the Copyright, Designs and Patents Act 1988.

All rights reserved. No part of this book may be reprinted or reproduced or utilized in any form or by any electronic, mechanical, or other means, now known or hereafter invented, including photocopying and recording, or in any information storage or retrieval system, without permission in writing from the publishers.

Trademark notice: Product or corporate names may be trademarks or registered trademarks, and are used only for identification and explanation without intent to infringe.

Library of Congress Cataloging-in-Publication Data
A catalog record for this title has been requested

ISBN: 978-0-367-33403-1 (hbk)
ISBN: 978-1-03-208327-8 (pbk)
ISBN: 978-0-429-31969-3 (ebk)

Typeset in Times New Roman
by Wearset, Boldon, Tyne and Wear

Contents

1	**Introduction**	1
2	**Theoretical Framework**	26

Social Provisioning 28
Institutional Economics 29
Social Philosophers 39

3	**How can the Hypothesis be Tested?**	46

PB in NYC Experience 47
Recommendations for Political Dimension 53
Conditions needed for Public Deliberation 56
Recommendations for Communicative Dimension 61
Implementation and Measurement 65

4	**Public Happiness**	73
5	**Increased Understanding of Others**	81

John Dewey 81
C. Wright Mills 82
Alfred Schutz 86

6	**Individual and Community Morality**	93

Ralph Waldo Emerson 94
Henry David Thoreau 96
Walt Whitman 99
John Dewey 103
C. Wright Mills 105
Port Huron Statement 106

vi *Contents*

7 A Sense of Belonging

114

The League of the Iroquois 114
C. Wright Mills 116
Julien Talpin 118
The Social Capital of Robert Putnam 119

8 Conclusion

127

Appendix

137

Index

138

1 Introduction

The purpose of this research monograph is to identify the potential benefits of participatory budgeting (PB), learn how they might be realized, and explore the implications of achieving these benefits. PB is a process where people gather in neighborhood assemblies to decide how to spend a portion of their municipal budget, which has proven to be successful and very popular since its invention in 1989 (Baiocchi & Ganuza, 2012). It is a form of local direct democracy. The PB process decides which public goods and services to purchase and how these goods and services will be distributed, within the bounds that city officials have authorized.

Since human beings are social beings, it makes sense that increasing our ability to work with and help others would be beneficial for both individuals and the community. This research explores how we might find our better selves by becoming empowered and actively engaged in public deliberations about local economic/political issues. It is proposed that this can be done by making improvements to PB.

The hypothesis of this research monograph is that as PB processes become more deliberative, more empowered, and greatly expanded the more participants will experience public happiness, greater understanding of others, greater development of morality, and an increased sense of belonging. It is proposed that PB processes be expanded until they become local direct democracies. This is a study about how the ideal of democracy can be achieved and how achieving this ideal can transform individuals, communities, and nations. The benefits of increased public happiness and greater development of morality are not expected to emerge until PB's responsibilities are greatly expanded.

PB is examined to learn how PB processes can fully realize its potential to transform individuals and increase its contribution to the social provisioning process. Many heterodox economists find the concept of social provisioning to be useful because it considers factors that are outside the scope of orthodox economics. Social provisioning expands on the orthodox definition of provisioning by including intangible benefits as well as the tangible benefits of food, clothing, and housing. In this case, the intangible benefits are increased public happiness, greater understanding of others, greater development of morality, and an increased sense of belonging.

2 Introduction

Institutional Economics is one school of thought in heterodox economics which is used to examine the PB process. One part of Institutional Economics is the theory of institutional adjustment, which explains how change occurs in institutions (Foster, 1981). In the case of PB, this theory points to the need to change the relationship between PB and city agencies in order to fully empower PB participants. The theory of institutional adjustment is based on the instrumental theory of value which provides criteria to make judgments by identifying what promotes harmonious relationships for individuals and provides for the communities' well-being. The methodology of this study is based on the concepts of social provisioning, philosophical research, and the Institutional Economics of Dewey and Foster, which are explained in Chapter 2.

The potential benefits in the hypothesis are examined in Chapters 4 though 7 by reviewing the relevant work of social philosophers, for each benefit, in order to gain a better perception of how these benefits can be realized and how they can change individuals' lives and community life. The social philosophers provide a vision of a better society and a better political system and show how it can be done. A clear vision will help people to commit to implementing a new social innovation such as transforming PB processes into local direct democracies.

Recommendations are made, in Chapter 3 that should allow PB assemblies to reach their full potential and develop into direct democracies. These recommendations are based on a case study of PB in New York City (PBNYC), an ethnographic study by Talpin of three European PB processes, and Foster's theory of institutional adjustment (Chapter 2). The benefits generated from improving PB should include increasing our public happiness, becoming more understanding of others, develop our morality, and increase our sense of belonging. Once the recommendations begin to be implemented the benefits should have transformative effects on individual participants regarding their social relationships and their sense of belonging to a community. This should cause participants to want to spend more time supporting PB by attending meetings. These benefits should increase participation though word of mouth as they begin to be realized.

The greater the participation in a PB process, the greater the percentage of the public will be voting on how to allocate the public goods and services that city officials have authorized the PB process to distribute. This means that the distribution of public goods and services will more closely reflect the will of the people. As PB participation increases, the PB process approaches the most democratic way to distribute public goods and services. When PB approaches its full potential, the benefits should become more apparent and further increase participation. Thus, as the potential benefits are realized the more democratic PB processes become.

This study proposes that the hypothesis can be tested by improving two areas of PB and measuring the results. The first one is political, which includes reorganizing the city's administrative bureaucratic hierarchy. PB participants will be further empowered to make decisions by placing the city's bureaucratic administrative offices under PB in the bureaucratic hierarchy in order to prevent bureaucratic priorities from superseding PB decisions. The other part of the political aspect is the need to greatly expand PB's funding and the range of projects and programs that PB is able to propose, authorize, and monitor. Both of these can be accomplished with the help of civic groups. The incentive for civic groups is that some, or all, of their priorities could be addressed in an expanded PB process. Civic groups can help mobilize people to peacefully demand that both of PB's political recommendations be implemented, which will help transform PB by empowering participants to make meaningful decisions. This is expected to be a long process because it will take time to convince city officials that these changes will benefit everyone.

Achieving the political aspect will transform PB processes into local direct democracies. This will allow participants to experience public happiness as they become the local government (see Chapter 4). Local direct democracy is a form of participatory democracy. And participatory democracy was the theme of the Port Huron Statement, which was the founding document for the Students for a Democratic Society (SDS). The SDS was successful in getting people to participate in peaceful demonstrations and raising awareness, which helped several social movements in the 1960s (see Chapter 6).

The other area in need of improvement is public communication. Improving public communication should benefit the individual participants as well as the community. The communicative aspect concerns improving public deliberation in the public forums by offering training for participants and facilitators. This is important because very little deliberation currently takes place at PB assemblies (Talpin, 2011). Open discussions among a diverse group of people will likely generate better ideas than experts and bureaucrats because people with different points of view will likely offer unexpected and novel ideas to be discussed. Public deliberation is also a good way to break down barriers between people resulting in better understanding of others and an increased sense of belonging to the community. In Chapter 5, Schutz's research showed that well-run public assemblies can promote understanding of others. In Chapter 7, Baiocchi's research looked at conditions in PB assemblies that resulted in participants having a sense of belonging.

The primary methodology of this study is philosophical research. The work of social philosophers is examined to learn how working toward the ideal of democracy will benefit individuals and communities. Chapters 4 through 7 comprise the philosophical research. One reason for the philosophical approach is that the ideal of democracy is a moral concept, since it is about treating everyone with dignity and respect by giving everyone an equal voice and an equal vote. Philosophy can do a good job of presenting moral choices as well as presenting the wisdom of different choices (Dewey, 1993). Chapter 2 presents additional information about the philosophical approach.

Next, the two areas of PB where recommendations are being made are further clarified. For the political area, an example is given of a successful PB process that had implemented a reorganization of the city's administrative organizations.

4 *Introduction*

For the communication aspect, the benefits of public deliberation are explored and an example of a deliberative society ruled by consensus is given.

One part of the political aspect was the need to reorganize the city's bureaucratic hierarchy to further empower participants. One might ask why this has not been done since PB was first invented in Brazil in 1989. The fact is that the first PB process in Porto Alegre, Brazil was designed with PB above other city bureaucracies within the administrative hierarchy.

Baiocchi and Ganuza outline part of the reason why Porto Alegre's PB was declared a "best practice" at the United Nations Habitat II meeting in 1996 (Baiocchi & Ganuza, 2017).

> The mayor [of Porto Alegre] created a budget planning office that centralized management accounts and PB; administratively it was positioned *above* municipal departments. The idea was to "ring-fence" the capital budget from other sources of pressure. By privileging the office above municipal departments, the administration ensured impartiality in implementation.
>
> (2017, p. 60)

The alternative to allowing the people to make local decisions is to allow experts within bureaucracies to make decisions. Later in this chapter the short-comings of expert bureaucratic rule are examined.

The other part of Porto Alegre's empowerment of PB was to ensure that PB received expert opinion from the bureaucracies before decisions were made.

> The administration required all municipal departments to create positions for community facilitators. Community facilitators were the "face" of each municipal department in each of the city's districts. They attended all PB meetings with the express purpose of helping participants prepare technically viable projects and to be accountable for ongoing projects. That is, they were responsible for interfacing between community and technical experts within the departments. All community facilitators attended a weekly forum to synthesize participatory processes.
>
> (Baiocchi & Ganuza, 2017, pp. 60–61)

While the bureaucracy was prevented from interfering with PB's decisions, they were required to help the PB process.

Unfortunately, PB in Porto Alegre might no longer be considered a best practice of local governance. The reason is that PB's invention and history were tied to the PT political party (Worker's Party) and in 2004 PT lost the local elections. The winning party did not consider PB to be a high priority and did not provide the needed support (Marquetti, da Silva, & Campbell, 2012).

It seems surprising that the PT party would have lost in Porto Alegre, since PB was such a success. "The reasons for the electoral defeat were not straightforward" (Baiocchi, 2005, p. 158). But it seems that the winning mayor (Fogaca) ran a well-organized campaign.

With respect to OP [PB] in particular, Fogaca cited administration materials about currently delayed projects and promised an improved and more responsive OP [PB]; unable to claim that a vote for the opposition was a vote against the OP [PB], the PT lost one of its trump cards in its bid for a fifth municipal term.

(Baiocchi, 2005, p. 158)

The PT party could not effectively use PB as a reason they should be re-elected. Thus, the lesson is that PB should not be connected to a political party. In North America a nonpolitical nonprofit organization, Participatory Budgeting Project, supports PB processes.

Why is it that the vast majority of PB processes around the world do not have this design feature concerning city bureaucracy? The answer is that the design of PB has evolved. Baiocchi and Ganuza find it useful to disaggregate PB into two components in order to better understand the process and explain how PB has travelled around the world.

We [Baiocchi and Ganuza] describe these two sides of participatory budgeting – participation and administrative reform – as the communicative and the sovereignty dimensions of PB. We use the term communicative dimension to describe the open structure of transparent meetings to deliberate on projects and priorities.

(Baiocchi & Ganuza, 2017, p. 141)

The sovereignty dimension describes the administrative reforms needed for city bureaucracies to be able to interact with the public and work with the PB process to develop new projects, while preventing bureaucrats from overruling PB (Baiocchi & Ganuza, 2017). The political dimension, as used in this study, includes the sovereignty dimension plus working to expand the amount of funding and the scope of projects and programs that the PB processes are able to authorize and monitor. Since PB has proven to be very popular, asking local politicians to strengthen and expand a popular program might not be as difficult as it seems.

The reason Baiocchi and Ganuza chose to examine PB in such a manner is that as PB has travelled the world, it has lost the sovereignty dimension. "The globally replicable version of participatory budgeting and its best practices had no elements of administrative reform, and PB was essentially reduced to a set of meetings" (Baiocchi & Ganuza, 2017, p. 71). One reason this has happened is because it is easier. "By not defining participation as part of the administration but as an external tool that influences it, it became much easier to implement" (Baiocchi & Ganuza, 2017, p. 76). This might be one reason PB has expanded so rapidly.

Another way that PB has changed is that it seems to have lost its social justice component. As PB travelled around the world it has become known as a tool of good governance. "Yet the process of translation from one context to another turned PB into an instrument abstracted from a political project altogether, one

6 *Introduction*

associated with the neutral idea of 'good governance'" (Baiocchi & Ganuza, 2017, p. 69). PB was just seen as a way to deliver city goods and services. This may have made PB easier to sell to a variety of governments.

How did PB transform into a value-neutral idea? The way PB is presented may have a lot to do with it. "The expert presentation of PB as value-neutral may feel necessary to introduce it in certain contexts, and this can narrow the grounds for reopening the discussion to speak for sovereignty reforms" (Baiocchi & Ganuza, 2017, p. 153). The experts may feel that a value-neutral PB is the best that certain countries can accept and implement.

> One of the changes with the global travel of PB has been the creation of *dedicated* PB networks (in which both authors [Baiocchi & Ganuza] have participated), which have tended over time to become dissociated from other discussions of participatory democracy or from discussions about cities and social justice.
>
> (Baiocchi & Ganuza, 2017, p. 154)

Thus, the way PB is presented is probably the way it will be implemented. And once again, this change made it easier for PB to expand. Of course, the easy way is not necessarily the best way.

The value aspect of PB is important because values provide a criteria of judgment when choices are made (Tool, 2000). As discussed in Chapter 2, values can define "what is" and "what ought to be." Without explicit values the implication is that everything is as it should be.

The PB experiment in Porto Alegre is a good example of including the political aspect in PB's design. The original PB process in Porto Alegre did seek to change things for the better. It was a political project. They sought to include the disenfranchised and provide goods and services to those neighborhoods who had not received their fair share. Two studies are reviewed to see how well this PB process performed.

> The Center for Urban Studies and Advising, CIDADE ... conducted research on the social and economic profiles of the PB participants in 1995, 1998, 2000, and 2002 ... The results show strong participation by traditionally underrepresented groups in three dimensions: income, education, and gender.
>
> (Marquetti et al., 2012, p. 69)

Thus, this experiment in local governance did attract the traditionally disenfranchised and marginalized groups, as intended.

To analyze the redistributive aspect, the authors of "Participatory Economic Democracy in Action: Participatory Budgeting in Porto Alegre, 1989–2004" examined data from the city of Porto Alegre and the official website of the PB, for the period 1990–2004. They found "a clear negative association between the average nominal income of the household head in the region and the number of

Introduction 7

demands per capita executed in the region. PB has a clear redistributive effect toward the economically disadvantaged" (Marquetti et al., 2012, p. 76). In other words, the lower the average income in a region, the higher the number of executed projects from PB.

There was one characteristic among participants found by the authors of the study, which might explain in part why PB in Porto Alegre was successful, connections participants had with other civil society organizations.

> 61.1 percent of [regional meeting] round attendees in 2002 participated in at least one organization … This connection transmits influences both ways: on the one hand it brings improved organizational capabilities to … poorly organized … groups, while on the other hand it solidly anchors the PB process in local concerns.
>
> (Marquetti et al., 2012, p. 71)

Additionally, it gave participants a chance to practice their deliberative skills outside the PB meetings.

PB participants should be encouraged to work with other civic groups for several reasons. First, it will enable people to have a bigger influence in their communities. Next, people working with multiple civic groups will gain a better understanding of their community and be in a better position to recommend positive changes in PB assemblies. And finally, doing so should increase the sense of belonging among the participants. Once the benefits of active participation become apparent, I believe that more people will find time to participate.

Many authors reported four important results from the PB process in Porto Alegre.

> The literature on PB … has emphasized four particular results. First, it supports the ideal of democracy … Second, it has a pedagogical effect in that participants learn about rights and responsibilities … Third, PB improves the fiscal performance of governments … Finally … it tends to improve the quality of life of the poor.
>
> (Marquetti et al., 2012, p. 63)

The fiscal performance is improved because a spotlight is put on the budget and everyone is able to participate in determining priorities. These are some of the reasons why PB has been growing rapidly around the world. The fact that PB supports the ideal of democracy supports the proposal of this research that changes should be made that will move PB closer to the democratic ideal.

The other part of PB that needs improvement is the public communication aspect. The recommendation is that public deliberation be encouraged by training participants and facilitators, which should provide many benefits for participants and the community. As was mentioned earlier, most PB processes currently have very little deliberation (Talpin, 2011). Before focusing on the

8 *Introduction*

values of public deliberation, it may be useful to briefly review the other ways policy is determined in a democracy.

> Deliberation represents one of three decision-making mechanisms in a democratic society: voting, bargaining, and arguing (deliberation) (Elster, 1998) ... [F]or both voting and bargaining, actors' preferences are seen as exogenous to the process itself. In contrast, deliberation relies on the endogenization of preferences.
>
> (Heller & Rao, 2015, p. 5)

In other words, neither voting nor bargaining affects individuals' preferences, which could be taken as given. But deliberation can change individuals' preferences, which can converge during the course of deliberation.

The opportunity for deliberation is at the heart of the PB process. It is what can happen in the PB assemblies after experts have informed the citizens about the specifics of a local issue which is on the agenda to be discussed. Jane Mansbridge defines deliberation in the public sphere as "mutual communication that involves weighing and reflecting on preferences, values, and interests regarding matters of common concern" (2015, p. 29). Mutual means two or more people need to be actively involved in communicating. The weighting and reflecting portion of the definition means careful thought is needed to reach a decision. The last portion of the definition, matters of common concern, specifies that the matter involve the entire group. Mansbridge (2015) says this is a minimalist definition because it does not include the standards to judge the quality of a deliberation, such as using persuasion and not coercion and showing mutual respect.

Deliberation is important for the creation and modification of societal values, which is important since we are constantly evolving based on new circumstances and new information.

> Public debates and discussions, permitted by political freedoms and civil rights, can also play a major part in the formation of values. Indeed, even the identification of needs cannot but be influenced by the nature of public participation and dialogue. Not only is the force of public discussion one of the correlates of democracy ... but its cultivation can also make democracy itself function better.
>
> (Sen, 2001, p. 158)

When democracy functions better, the government is more responsive to the needs of the people. And these needs are more clearly defined due to deliberation.

Deliberation may not lead to consensus, but it can bring us closer to an agreement, in the following four ways.

> First ... it can reduce the degree to which manipulation, deception, and propaganda inevitably seep into any communicative situation.

Introduction 9

Second, deliberation can provide new information ...

Third ... it can facilitate coordination ...

Fourth ... as participants gain greater understanding of others, they are more likely to take others' preferences or moral worldviews into account.

(Heller & Rao, 2015, p. 7)

Thus, deliberation can help clarify, inform, foster collaboration, and promote empathy.

Another reason that deliberation is important is that the procedures needed to make deliberation work are a good way to counteract inequality.

But even if formal political equality prevails in many democracies in the developing world, inequalities of agency and associational capacity remain the norm. In thinking through the possibilities for deliberation, one has to begin from a position of skepticism: making deliberation work calls for specific processes, practices, and institutional designs that can level or at least neutralize associational inequalities.

(Heller & Rao, 2015, p. 15)

Doing the work of enabling deliberation gives voice to those who have had no voice. This is true not only for developing countries, but for developed countries as well. "This is a challenge that is faced both by well-established democracies such as the United States (especially with the differential participation of diverse racial groups) and by newer democracies" (Sen, 2001, p. 159). Inequality is pervasive around the world, and deliberation is a good counter measure. In Chapter 3, changes to the rules, procedures, and practices of PB are proposed that should help counteract inequality, encourage more deliberation, empower participants, and increase participation. And as explained in Chapters 5 and 7, public deliberation can help increase understanding of others and create a greater sense of belonging to the community.

Public deliberation can work in today's extremely polarized political environment. "Deliberation can overcome polarization ... In deliberative conditions, the group becomes less extreme; absent deliberative conditions, the members become more extreme" (Dryzek et al., 2019, p. 1145). People can come together when see each other as human beings that deserve dignity and respect.

Nearly everyone agrees that the ideal of public deliberation has several benefits for everyone who participates. However, is it possible for people to publicly deliberate and decide all local issues? The League of the Iroquois is a confederation of American Indian tribes that demonstrates that a deliberative society is not only possible but can thrive. This confederation of tribes is examined in Chapter 7. But, can a modern society transition into a modern deliberative society? "The real world of democratic politics is currently far from the deliberative ideal, but empirical evidence shows that the gap can be closed" (Dryzek et al., 2019,

10 *Introduction*

p. 1144). Since the gap can be closed, it is imperative that the work is done to encourage and maintain public deliberation.

It seems likely that improving these two aspects of PB would have beneficial results for individuals and communities. However, why should we spend the time and energy now? The answer is that the trend of far right populist authoritarian leaders gaining power around the world is threatening democracy.

The rise of far right populist authoritarian leaders has been a troubling trend around the world. "The far right party family is the fastest-growing party family in Europe" (Golder, 2016, p. 477). However, they are not controlling the majority of European countries. "Since the current European crisis, Poland and Hungary … have experienced substantial back sliding with the latter perhaps even having fully regressed to authoritarianism" (Bernhard & O'Neill, 2018, p. 595). The growth of far right authoritarian parties is significant.

> Across Europe, the average share of the vote won by these parties for the lower house in national parliamentary elections in Europe has more than doubled since the 1960s, from around 5.4 percent to 12.4 percent today. During the same era, their share of seats has tripled, from 4.0 percent to 12.2 percent.
>
> (Norris & Inglehart, 2019, p. 9)

Of course, this is not just happening in Europe.

Far right populist authoritarian leaders are becoming commonplace. "From Turkey and Hungary, to India and the Philippines, the voices of nationalism and the far right have become dominant forces that begin with the election of a charismatic, influential and powerful man" (Gogoi, 2019, p. 2). An example is what has happened in Hungary. "It [Orban's party in Hungary] whittled down the power of courts, changed how elections are supervised and dramatically curbed media" (Gogoi, 2019, p. 3). It appears to be common practice for the elected authoritarian leader to attack democratic institutions that are meant to contain and limit the chief executive's power such as a free press and independent judges. In the Philippines, President Duterte has killed "thousands of alleged drug dealers across the country. Human rights groups say the innocent poor have borne the brunt of these killings" (Gogoi, 2019, p. 3). Basic human rights suffer when these leaders come to power. And most recently, Brazil has also elected a far right populist authoritarian leader. "Jair Bolsonaro, Brazil's new president, is among a wave of far-right leaders who have risen on the world stage" (Gogoi, 2019, p. 1). These examples make it clear that democratic institutions, democratic values, and democracy itself is under attack. Many of the far right leaders campaign on traditional moral values. I would argue that treating all citizens with dignity and respect is based on traditional morality and traditional democratic values.

Trump became one of the far right populist authoritarian leaders after he won the election in 2016 to become the President of the United States. Trump uses populist rhetoric "promoting authoritarian values that threaten the liberal norms underpinning American democracy … Trump's angry nativist speeches, anti-establishment appeals, and racially heated language resembles that of many other leaders whose support has been swelling across Europe" (Norris & Inglehart, 2019, p. 1). Of course, Trump is not the first anti-immigrant politician in the United States. "Historically, right-wing movements in the United States have been highly xenophobic and nationalist, working to stop immigration of non-whites through law, force, and violence (Blee 1991, Flint 2004b, McVeigh 2009, Zeskind 2009)" (Blee & Creasap, 2010, p. 275). These types of tactics seem to be for the purpose of creating a common enemy that populist politicians use to rally their followers. "Nativism combines nationalism with xenophobia in that it calls for states to comprise members of the native group and considers non-native elements to be fundamentally threatening to the monocultural nation-state (Mudde 2007, p. 19)" (Golder, 2016, p. 480). The people who can be excluded from humane treatment and basic human rights are treated as the enemy. They are primarily foreigners but not necessarily. "Non-native elements are identified on the basis of cultural traits such as race, ethnicity, or religion, and can include minorities from within the native ethic group, such as homosexuals" (Golder, 2016, p. 480). Minorities who are identified as being different are used by far right populist authoritarian leaders to gain, and maintain, power.

"Rightist movements tend to be known for what they are against, not for what they support (Durham 2007, Lo 1982)" (Blee & Creasap, 2010, p. 271). Other than being anti-immigrant, one of the most common groups they are against seems to be sexual minorities. "A particular focus was sexual minorities (Burack 2008, Fetner 2008, Richardson 2006, Stein 2001)" (Blee & Creasap, 2010, p. 274). The authoritarian leaders seem to regard them as especially dangerous. Of course, there is no evidence to fear sexual minorities. However, the populist rhetoric of these leaders is able to invoke fear, anger, and hatred against groups that are identified as being different.

How did far right populist authoritarian leaders become such a trend? "Two contending explanations for the rise of the right can be found in literature: One emphasizes the *economic reasons* [economic insecurity], and the other *cultural values* [cultural backlash] behind the electorate's motivation to support far-right parties" (Ausserladscheider, 2019, p. 1). The economic insecurity thesis believes that people who feel they have been left behind by globalization are more likely to vote for the far right. "For many decades, the explanation for the rise of the far right was seen in economic grievances such as increasing inequality, dysfunctional markets, the overall perception of the economy, and an individual's economic status" (Ausserladscheider, 2019, p. 1). Both income and wealth inequality have been rising for decades (Galbraith, 2009). However, although the economic insecurity hypothesis seems reasonable, it may not be the primary reason for the rise of authoritarian leaders. "Mudde's analysis [Mudde, 2007] similarly confirms the cultural backlash thesis by arguing that economic programmes in right-wing populism are merely adjuncts to a bigger reaction to progressive values" (Ausserladscheider, 2019, p. 7). While economic insecurity may play a part in the support for the far right, it seems that cultural backlash is the most popular reason to support the far right.

12 Introduction

The cultural backlash seems to have started in the 1960s and 1970s. "Right-wing populism is often seen as a direct response to the counter-culture revolution of the 1960s and 1970s in Europe" (Siegel, 2017, p. 2), which is why the far right populist authoritarian leaders talk about cultural issues. "[T]oday's radical conservatism is also the product of a decades-long attempt to craft a philosophical position capable of mounting an intellectual challenge to the contemporary liberal order, fostering political movements dedicated to its destruction" (Drolet & Williams, 2018, p. 286). The 1960s was a time of social movements changing the cultural norms. "[P]ostmateralist values [from the 1960s and 1970s] prioritize the expansion of individual freedom and emphasize things such as multiculturalism, gender and racial equality, and sexual freedom" (Golder, 2016, p. 483). The conservatives started a decades' long effort to reverse these values. "[T]he New Right (NR) emerged in the 1970s, a time when the right had little electoral or cultural influence" (Blee & Creasap, 2010, p. 272). These new conservatives focused on cultural issues. "While earlier forms of conservatism emphasized fiscal sobriety, the backlash mobilizes voters with explosive social issues – summoning public outrage over everything from busing to un-Christian art – which it then marries to pro-business economic policies" (Frank, 2005, p. 5). Conservatives were voting only, or primarily, on the cultural issues. "[V]oters increasingly endorse single-issue movements" (Foa & Mounk, 2016, p. 6).

> In fact, backlash leaders systematically downplay the politics of economics. The movement's basic premise is that culture outweighs economics as a matter of public concern … [B]ut once conservatives are in office the only old-fashioned situation they care to revive is an economic regimen of low wages and lax regulations.
>
> (Frank, 2005, p. 6)

It is ironic that people voted for the cultural issues and received laissez-faire policies favored by big business. "In many cases, these [far right] parties blur their actual economic position in an attempt to maintain a cross-class coalition of support (Rovny 2013)" (Golder, 2016, p. 490). It is easier to campaign to a diverse population if you do not specify the party's actual economic position. "Thus, the primary contradiction of the backlash: it is a working-class movement that has done incalculable, historic harm to working-class people" (Frank, 2005, p. 6). In many cases, people vote against their own economic best interests.

Because conservatives were framing cultural issues as moral issues, religion became a natural ally. "[R]eligion became a powerful force for mobilizing new constituencies on the right in the 1980s as evangelical Christians sought to 'evangelize and organize' by building pressure groups such as the Moral Majority and Focus on the Family (Jacobs 2006, p. 360)" (Blee & Creasap, 2010, p. 273). Once in office, the politicians could then vote for policies favoring their core constituency – big business. Changing cultural values is an issue that may never go away because change seems to be the only constant in modern life, including changing values.

Introduction 13

Historically, religion has been slow to adopt new knowledge, norms, and values. Thus, religion has slowed society's acceptance of instrumentally verified knowledge and in some cases have sought legislation to impose their views on others. This politicization of religion has been used by far right authoritarian leaders to legitimize themselves and their anti-democratic agenda.

The rise of populist authoritarian leaders is an indication that the current representative democracies are not working as intended. "The share of citizens who approve of 'having a strong leader who does not have to bother with parliament or elections,' for example has gone up markedly in most countries where the World Values Survey asked the question" (Foa & Mounk, 2017, pp. 6–7). Some people have lost faith in modern democracy with its checks and balances.

> Authoritarian values blended with populist rhetoric can be regarded as a dangerous combination fueling a cult of fear. Populist rhetoric directs tribal grievance 'upwards' toward elites, feeding mistrust of 'corrupt' politicians, the 'fake' media, 'biased' judges, and 'out-of-touch' mainstream parties, assaulting the truth and corroding faith in liberal democracy.
>
> (Norris & Inglehart, 2019, p. 7)

Thus, authoritarian populism further weakens democracy by attacking the credibility of democratic institutions such as a free press and independent judges, as noted earlier. However, there is evidence that some people are holding on to democratic norms. "Surveys consistently show that many Europeans hold anti-immigrant attitudes, and yet relatively few vote for far right parties. Blinder et al. (2013) suggest that this is due to a widespread norm against prejudice and discrimination" (Golder, 2016, p. 485).

The far right's strongest supporters are in the older generation.

> Cultural grievances are particularly strong among the older generation of white conservatives, the people most likely to feel disoriented by the rapid transformation of their societies. The evidence suggests that rapidly growing racial and ethnic diversity, not immigration per se, is most closely associated with authoritarian values.
>
> (Norris & Inglehart, 2019, p. 456)

The far right is against diversity. They seem to want to be able to exclude minorities who have different cultural values. The argument in favor of diversity is that people with different cultural backgrounds will likely have different perspectives on social issues, which could help solve social problems.

Differences in gender, race, ethnic background, or country of origin are superficial. In Chapter 6, Walt Whitman's views are examined. Concerning diversity, Whitman believed that we are all born with the same potentials and it is only individual circumstances that cause individuals to take different pathways through life. Whitman believed that we are all much more alike than we are different (Whitman, 1982). Since we are all human beings it makes sense that

14 *Introduction*

we should try to work with different groups of people who may have different interests.

Populism rejects the idea of pluralism where different groups have different interests. "Populism desires that power be placed in the unfettered hands of the people, and calls for the increased use of referenda, popular initiatives, and direct executive elections.... [I]ts proponents see themselves as the defenders of true democracy" (Golder, 2016, p. 483). However, referendums and initiatives are just yes or no votes by the people without any organized public deliberation before the vote. Referendums and popular initiatives fall short of the standards for deliberative democracy, which would require careful consideration of how a proposed law is worded and consideration of all possible effects.

An example of a far right referendum is Brexit. This was the 2016 vote by British citizens to leave the European Union (EU). The EU is an economic and political union promoting the well-being of its member states. Because there were no formal deliberations before the vote, which would have happened in a legislative body such as Parliament, or the deliberative public forums proposed in this research, the result seems to be a train wreck that is slowly happening as we watch. "Even the leaders of Leave camp seemed surprised by the outcome as they admitted they had no plan for what 'Brexit' would look like" (Hobolt, 2016, p. 1259). The problem is that EU agreements effect many aspects of the British economy. And abruptly cutting all ties to the EU would be a severe negative shock to the British economy and to a lesser degree negatively impact the EU economy. The people who campaigned to stay in the EU, the Remain camp, thought they would win because there was "an overwhelming consensus among experts that a Brexit outcome would have negative economic consequences for Britain" (Hobolt, 2016, p. 1262). However, the emotional arguments of the far right persuaded people to vote against their own economic best interests.

The arguments of the Leave camp were anti-immigration, anti-establishment, and anti-culturalism (Hobolt, 2016).

> Concerns about the cultural and economic threats of globalization, immigration and European integration are effectively mobilized by parties, especially on the populist right, that have been gaining ground in national and European elections (see Hobolt and De Vries 2015, 2016b; Van Elsas et al. 2016).
>
> (Hobolt, 2016, p. 1260)

Notice that part of the successful leave campaign was based on economics in spite of the experts saying that leaving would have negative economic consequences. The far right dismisses expert and scientific conclusions when it is their best interests to do so.

The question of European integration, or Euroscepticism, was framed by the Leave camp "as a chance for ordinary citizens to 'take back control' from the élites in Brussels [headquarters of the EU]" (Hobolt, 2016, p. 1264). The élites are a common target for the far right. They are depicted as being responsible for the changing, or declining, morality. European élites are seen as having "shared socially liberal values, respecting diversity, social tolerance and trust, equality of opportunity for women and ethnic minorities, and the protection of minority rights" (Norris & Inglehart, 2019, p. 193). This is very similar to views that the Republican party in the United States have about intellectuals and the "liberal élite" (Frank, 2005).

Concerning European integration, this is part of a larger issue the far right has with global governance. The far right fears that various global governance institutions will create new norms. These institutions include the following:

> international law (really transnational law); transnational courts such as the International Criminal Court; myriad UN conventions that establishes new global norms, particularly in the area of human rights; supranational institutions like the EU; and non-government organizations (NGOs) that act as "global civil society".
>
> (Drolet, 2010, p. 539)

The far right believes that supranational institutions do, or could, interfere with duties that nation-states need to perform.

> [T]he neo-conservative vision of America ... maintain[s] that the cultural revolutions of the 1960s and the ensuing "tragedy of multiculturalism" have forever disturbed the consensus on the values of the majority culture that have for so long contained class and racial conflicts and made American capitalist democracy possible.
>
> (Drolet, 2010, 552)

The far right does not want supranational institutions to enact laws protecting the rights of minority cultures.

Somehow, the far right believes that taking rights away from minority cultures will make minorities easier to control, which is somehow in the best interest of the majority. In the eyes of the far right, the emerging global governance would "deprive the Right from a key site of political mobilisation in its effort to roll back multiculturalism, re-moralise the social contract and contain the debilitating effects of cultural modernity" (Drolet, 2010, p. 554). The far right is against multiculturalism because it would mean respecting and providing equal rights for everyone. This would be antithetical to all far right authoritarian leaders around the world. "Indeed, for the NR [New Right], the very idea of international human rights developing towards and around purportedly universal principles ... forecloses the legitimacy of 'native' definitions of values or rights" (Drolet & Williams, 2018, p. 299). As defined earlier, native for the far right means excluding groups. Groups that have been excluded from native definitions include foreigners. Groups born within the country may also be excluded due to race, religion, sexual orientation, or gender identification. "[R]ight-wing variants [extremists] view inequality as part of the natural order and not something that

16 *Introduction*

should be subject to state intervention (Mudde 2007)" (Golder, 2016, p. 479). Human rights for all human beings would prevent authoritarian leaders from demonizing groups for the sake of political power or any other reason. Human rights for everyone is a democratic norm.

How could anyone expect to prevail in attempts to revitalize democracy in the face of such leaders who distort, exaggerate, and lie in order to play on the people's misconceptions, fears, and prejudges? These tactics can be overcome whenever the people discover a passion for a vision of a better life, which could result from the proposal in this research. Next, Dewey's insights concerning the internal deliberation of individuals is examined to learn why people may change their habits of thought and why emotions and passion is a key to change.

One of Dewey's insights was that habits govern nearly everything that we do on a daily basis. Even our thought is submerged in habit (Dewey, 2002). "Without habit there is only irritation and confused hesitation" (Dewey, 2002, p. 180). Habits allow us to brush aside thoughts of little decisions we are faced with each day while we do our jobs, interact with our friends and family, and perform our necessary chores.

And once habits are formed, by definition they tend to persist. "Habits once formed perpetuate themselves" (Dewey, 2002, p. 125). Habits become comfortable and allow us to live our lives.

The question is how we change our habit of thinking? Dewey wrote, "impulse operates as a pivot, or reorganization of habit" (Dewey, 2002, p. 156). It is a way to temporary interrupt the routine.

> The release of some portion of the stock of impulses is an opportunity, not an end. In its origin, it is the product of chance; but it affords imagination and invention their chance. The moral correlate of liberated impulse is not immediate activity, but reflection upon the way in which to use impulse to renew disposition and reorganizing habit.
>
> (Dewey, 2002, p. 170)

The release of impulse allows us time to reflect and possibly act in a new way. This new response may become a new habit.

Our social institutions help shape our social customs. Dewey writes that "social customs are not direct and necessary consequences of specific impulses, but that social institutions and expectations shape and crystallize impulses into dominant habits" (Dewey, 2002, p. 122). If impulses are released during PB assemblies, the PB assembly could help shape new habits of community discourse. Perhaps people can stop thinking of themselves primarily as individuals and start thinking of themselves primarily as members of the community.

The interruption of habit is due to "an excess of preferences, not natural apathy or an absence of likings" (Dewey, 2002, p. 193). This could be due to being presented with new ways of thinking about community issues during PB assemblies. Or emotional responses could be due to hearing about the plight of the less fortunate in the community. It can help change a delegate's habit of only voting for projects in her neighborhood, if another neighborhood is more in need. Emotions can lead to good and reasonable decisions. If people think that PB processes can be improved and expanded resulting in the benefits of the hypothesis being realized then maybe the thought of being a part of it will stir emotions and energize people into action.

It is not the case that emotionless evaluation is needed to create good changes in our behavior. "The conclusion is not that the emotional, passionate phase of action can be or should be eliminated in behalf of a bloodless reason. More 'passions,' not fewer, is the answer" (Dewey, 2002, pp. 195–196). Passions that conflict with our habits cause us to pause and reflect on staying with a habit of thought, or a habit of doing, versus changing a habit of thought or a habit of doing something. Once people realize all the benefits that are possible from becoming actively involved in local democracy, they may become open to, and passionate about, the possibility especially when they can begin slowly by attending PB meeting.

The proposal in this monograph is expected to be a slow process of people learning how to deliberate, seeing the benefits of deliberation, and then volunteering to help convince city leaders to give the PB process greater responsibilities and greater autonomy in decision-making. It does not matter how long the project takes. After all, democracy is a never-ending process.

Self-reflection is the key to change. One of the key benefits of public deliberation is that it can provoke self-reflection among the participants, which can result in changing one's views. "Deliberation promotes considered judgement and counteracts populism. In contrast to knee-jerk responses to partisan and populist cues, deliberation leads judgements to become more considered and more consistent with values that individuals find that they hold after reflection" (Dryzek et al., 2019, p. 1145). The Transcendentalists were a group of American philosophers who believed that self-reflection was a way to connect with God, which is why they believed that self-reflection was the way to improve one's self. Dewey's insight was that emotions and passions interrupt habitual patterns of thought leading to self-reflection with the possibility of changing habitual patterns of thought and action.

Before this study proceeds with explanations of the methodologies used (Chapter 2) and specific recommendations for changes (Chapter 3), it may be useful to examine some fundamentals about PB. First, it was invented in Brazil in 1989 and has become a worldwide movement that is now used in over 1,500 cities around the globe (Baiocchi & Ganuza, 2012). PB is a new phenomenon that is difficult to analyze because almost every PB process is different, in some way, from every other. PB processes are different due to motivations of local politicians in supporting PB, strength (or weakness) of local civic groups, degree of support from local governments, different histories of local communities, and the goals of local processes. The rapid growth of PB has resulted in a variety of rules, practices, and procedures being used with a corresponding assortment of results.

In addition to the reasons given earlier, the design of PB varies widely because, "[t]here is no recognized definition of participatory budgeting, either

18   *Introduction*

political or scientific, explaining the minimum criteria they must satisfy" (Sintomer, Herzberg, Röcke, & Allegretti, 2012, p. 2), in order to call themselves PB. Of course, there has been disagreement over what should be called PB.

PB was invented to bring the traditionally disenfranchised into the political process and allow the participants to distribute public goods and services to the neighborhoods most in need. Even though most PB processes around the world only distribute a small percentage of their city's budget, PB has proven to be very popular. People want to decide for themselves. Most people seem to believe in the democratic ideals of equality, an equal vote for everyone, and an equal voice for everyone.

There are two related ways that PB transcends the traditional liberal concept of democracy. The first is that by participating, people are engaging in a learning process during which some of their preferences will likely change, because they come to see issues from the perspectives of others. Second, as people develop their skills in debate and compromise, they experience a desire to do more (Marquetti et al., 2012). As people become better negotiators, they become more effective, which increases their satisfaction and their desire to do more.

PB helps to build the social fabric of a community by encouraging residents to discuss, debate, and decide capital improvement budget issues. Putnam referred to social networks as social capital, which can be used to help individuals and groups (2000). These social ties can be used to help people in the community accomplish goals. When it works well, a virtuous cycle can be created which means that when social networks accomplish their goals, the social networks are strengthened, which means they can accomplish more, which further strengthens the networks and so on. PB provides the space people need to make connections with each other and build the social networks needed to accomplish local political goals.

In Brazil, typically entire cities are organized in the PB process. At the base are neighborhood assemblies which elect representatives to regional meetings. Committees at the regional level develop proposals to be voted on. Since PB is not a legislative body, any projects approved through the PB process have to be voted on by elected representatives in the traditional way. The regions elect representatives to the Municipal Budget Council, which oversees the municipal PB process and makes a final budget recommendation to the city (Wampler, 2007b).

This description is a very high level overview of how PB works in many cities in Brazil. There are almost as many variations and permutations of the original Porto Alegre model as there are implementations of the PB process. Every municipality writes its own rules and procedures based on its perceived needs and historical experiences.

The PB process is new to the United States. It has been implemented in parts of Chicago and New York City, in several communities on the west coast, and in a few other cities. Each city writes its own rules concerning exactly how the process works, such as what projects are eligible and the timing of the annual budget cycle. In Chicago, each alderman has a discretionary budget for capital infrastructure projects which is used to provide funding for PB.[1] Of course, the

Introduction 19

same restrictions that apply to the alderman, such as the type of projects that may be funded, also apply to the PB process. The neighborhood assemblies are where brainstorming sessions for possible projects occur. Budget committees are formed for each thematic area such as public safety, transportation, and parks. The delegates to the budget committees are self-selected from the participants in the assemblies. Each committee works with the appropriate city agencies to develop concrete budget proposals from the ideas generated in the assemblies. The proposals are summarized on poster boards and displayed for public viewing with members of the budget committees available for questions. The community votes on the proposals, and the most popular ones are funded. In an effort to increase voter participation, people need not be registered to vote, nor do they need to be United States citizens. They just need to live in the community and be at least 16 years of age (Lerner, 2014).

For all PB processes around the world, civil society is important because it can help to institutionalize the means for citizens to become empowered and engage in a deliberative process of deciding economic/political issues – issues that are usually decided within the political society. Civil society organizations can help by being willing and able to engage in both cooperative and contentious forms of politics in order to extend the scope of authority of the PB process (Wampler, 2007a). Organized groups need to continue to advocate for the PB process, even after it has been established, to ensure that the process will succeed in the face of changing circumstances and changing power dynamics. Civic society can provide the space needed for the PB process to operate and possibly expand.

In *The Roots of Participatory Democracy* (Williams, 2008), the phrase "civil society" is used in two ways. First, civil society is the sphere of social organizations that is separate from, but connected with the state and the economy. Second, civil society is the sphere of voluntary associational activity where a great deal of daily life is experienced (Williams, 2008). It is important to recognize that civic society is not formally part of government and economic institutions and that it can remain relatively free of their influences and control. Civic society thus can remain free to advocate for neighborhood interests. The fact that civic society is entwined in daily life is the source of its potential power.

In order for the PB process to function well, it is important to achieve an appropriate balance between the aggregate reasoning of political society and the deliberative reasoning of civil society, There is a divide in the democracy literature between aggregating individual preferences which are taken as given and deliberative theorists who believe "people will modify their perceptions of what society should do in the course of discussing this with others" (Milner & Katznelson 2002, p. 237). Neoclassical economic theory takes individual preferences as given. Also, many scholars in Political Science believe that the role of government is to aggregate individual preferences. However, taking individual preferences as given does not allow for changing priorities and instead tends to lock in a snapshot of preferences. Deliberative theorists are concerned with getting people to engage each other with the goal of converging to the common

20   *Introduction*

good (Milner & Katznelson, 2002). Society's values and preferences change over time. And deliberative theorists believe encouraging people to deliberate is the best way to discover these preferences. Finding a balance between aggregating individual preferences and continuous public deliberation of preferences would maintain stability while providing a mechanism to clarify and define changing values and priorities, in light of new information and better perception.

The aggregate reasoning of political society and the deliberative reasoning of civil society may not always be mutually reinforcing, but may be in tension with each other. The political establishment may not wish to share their power. Or the public may not be willing or able to work within the existing political system. The capacity of citizens can be understood by examining the relationship between political and civil society (Heller, 2009).

The capacity of citizens may be increased by ensuring effective deliberation in the PB process. Effective deliberation has the tendency to reduce inequality. Pervasive inequality may prevent some groups from effectively engaging with the government. This certainly excludes some groups from deliberating in the PB process (Heller, 2009). "A high degree of consolidated representative democracy as we find in India and South Africa should not be confused with a high degree of effective citizenship" (Heller, 2009, p. 125). The ineffectiveness of their civil societies prevents them from being able to overcome this obstacle. The legal rights of people should not be confused with the capacity to participate in political or civil society.

Baiocchi and Ganuza (2012) believed the success of PB in being designated as an international "best practice," by the United Nations, has led to less reliance on civil society. This was the source of strength for the initial implementations of PB. As was mentioned previously, an important role of civil society is to advocate for the PB process. The lack of an engaged civil society results in PB processes that have less authority. "In Europe, for example, most experiences are advisory with the exception of Spain" (Baiocchi & Ganuza, 2012, p. 9). Of course, that is not to say that these new PB processes do not benefit the participants or the communities. However, the most successful PB processes have combined the institutional capacities of the state with the associational resources of civil society (Heller, 2001). Civil society involvement results in a more robust PB process.

Next, to be fair, detractors of PB should be given due consideration. Any debate about policy issues needs to examine all relevant viewpoints. The following looks at the most common arguments people have against the need for PB processes.

There seem to be two main objections to PB. The first is that elected officials are better qualified and better informed. Thus, they should be allowed to do the job for which they were elected without interference from PB assemblies. The second argument is that the management of the city and its neighborhoods should be left to the experts.

The first argument against the need for PB is that elected officials should be allowed to do their job because they are best able to do it. This argument is

Introduction 21

based on the belief that our current pluralist democracy is working well. The argument for pluralism "starts from two basic assumptions" (Greenberg, 1983, p. 31). The first assumption is that the citizens of the United States are not up to the task of getting directly involved. In other words, "citizens of the United States do not measure up to the standards set by theorists of democracy" (Greenberg, 1983, p. 31).

> Contemporary social science research demonstrates that most Americans are uninformed about politics and are neither overly interested nor particularly sophisticated about political events. Most Americans feel little compulsion to lend their energies to public affairs given the attraction of private pursuits.
>
> (Greenberg, 1983, p. 31)

Even if most Americans wanted to participate directly, most Americans do not have the knowledge to make well informed decisions.

The second assumption supporting the idea of a pluralist democracy is that our current political system works. "It [the American political system] not only provides for a peaceful transfer of power between ruling groups but for a method whereby the voices of all groups with interests in government policy are heard and considered" (Greenberg, 1983, p. 32). The system seems to work well enough.

If the two assumptions are correct, then political apathy fulfills a needed function in our society. If most people actively participate, the voice of the people will likely supersede the influence of the special interests, who are informed and interested in the system. Our political system would be influenced by people who are largely uninformed and disinterested. "We should be thankful for this [political apathy], because it is primarily among the mass public that we find intolerance and extremism" (Greenburg, 1983, p. 32). If most people did actively participate, we could be in worse shape.

A counterargument to the first assumption is that people can develop an interest in local politics and can learn about policy proposals during public deliberations. "[M]oreover, 'those most willing to deliberate are precisely those who are turned off by standard partisan and interest group politics' (7)" (Dryzek et al., 2019, p. 1145). Thus, making public deliberation available would likely appeal to a great many people. Also, public deliberation with trained PB facilitators should help people to arrive at reasonable solutions by helping to ensure that everyone is heard and by encouraging deliberation to take place. This is based on the belief that people want what is best for their own communities.

Concerning the second assumption, while it is true that our current pluralist democracy allows special interest groups to have a say in government, the theme of this study is that enabling PB to reach its full potential will benefit individual participants as well as the community, which should increase participation in PB. This would enrich our democracy by encouraging participation and cooperation. Also, it is assumed that governance will improve as more people deliberate policy issues. At the least, governance should more closely reflect the will of the people.

22 *Introduction*

The second argument that there is not a need for PB is that we should leave the management of our cities and neighborhoods to the experts. The logic of this argument is easy to see. Modern life is complicated and perhaps experts would make better decisions than ordinary citizens.

In the United States, there is an ideology that is closely related to expert rule. "Managerialism is an ideology, one that emphasizes technique and process above all else....Its thrust is toward efficiency and objectivity" (Skidmore, 1993, p. 191). And democracy, especially deliberative democracy, is very time consuming. Thus, democracy is inefficient. And of course, politics is messy.

The Progressive reformers saw managerialism as a way to clean up local governments.

> The Progressive reformers sought to break the power of the bosses. Because the support of the voters was the source of a boss's power, it followed that it was necessary to restrict the rule of the voter, at least of the voter who was likely to support the boss.
>
> (Skidmore, 1993, p. 212)

This ideology, which seeks to separate administration from policy, has proven to be popular.

> Merit-based bureaucracies to administer government service reflect the ideology, at least to some extent. Such bureaucracies are widespread, especially in industrial countries. Moreover, in the United States the highly popular council-manager form of city government is an attempt to ensure city administration by expert professionals. Initially at least, the council-manager movement also was an explicit attempt to remove entire governments as far from politics as possible.
>
> (Skidmore, 1993, p. 196)

But many times, it may be impossible to separate administration from policy. "In fact, the contention that policy and administration may be separated dates from the early theorists of public administration, and modern theory recognizes that it is impossible to separate the two completely" (Skidmore, 1993, p. 195). Thus, the result of managerialism is that we become less democratic, which means that the people are no longer involved in decisions about many issues that directly affect their lives.

The question, at this point is, will managerialism continue to be popular, or will it evolve into a more democratic form?

> With good will and effort, bureaucracy, technology, and an emphasis upon efficiency can be made compatible with human values. When and if this occurs, they will have proved a boon to humanity. If it fails to occur, managerialism will have prevailed and will have contributed greatly to the development of a dehumanized society.
>
> (Skidmore, 1993, p. 217)

An extreme type of managerialism would be the appointment of one person who does not answer to the voters or to local elected officials to run a city government.

Several states have passed laws that enable the governor to appoint an emergency manager, in the case of a fiscal emergency, to run a city.

> Worried that ailing cities were a threat to the state's credit rating, the Michigan legislature passed the Local Government and School District Fiscal Accountability Act. The Act allows cities to be placed in receivership if their economic health indicators are sufficiently dismal ... Once the city is in receivership, the Act invests the receiver – what the law terms the "emergency manager" – with nearly unlimited authority ... Perhaps the most troubling aspect of the law is that the receiver is free to continue in his position until he alone is satisfied that the financial emergency has receded.
>
> (Kossis, 2012, p. 111)

The idea is that one person, not responsible to the voters, can get things done that an elected mayor and city council were unable to do. "Most receivers do things that were previously debated and rejected by the city, such as cutting services, raising taxes, or firing public employees" (Kossis, 2012, p. 1135). The perception, apparently, is that the solutions to a city's financial troubles are always known, and it just takes a complete outsider from city politics to have the courage to take the unpopular, but needed, actions.

An example of the results of the emergency manager law can be seen in Flint, Michigan. The emergency manager, isolated from local accountability, decided to save money by changing the source of the city's water supply from the Detroit water system to corrosive river water, which leached lead from the pipes.

> Flint, led at the time by an emergency manager who was appointed by the state to help solve the city's fiscal woes, switched water supplies in April 2014 – in part to save money, which the emails [emails released by the governor's office 1/2016] showed amounted to $1 million to $2 million a year.
>
> (Bosman, Davey & Smith, 2016, p. 3)

The emergency manager risked the lives of Flint residents by making this decision. He chose to move toward balancing the budget in spite of the risk to human life. A democratic process would, most likely, have insisted on extensive multiple studies to guarantee the safety of the drinking water. The safety of the children would have been given priority over the budget.

Note

1 In New York City, some city council members allow PB to use their discretionary capital budget for their district.

24 *Introduction*

References

Ausserladschelder, V. (2019). Beyond economic insecurity and cultural backlash: Economic nationalism and the rise of the far right. *Sociology Compass, 13*(4). doi: 10.1111/soc4.12670

Baiocchi, G. (2005). *Militants and citizens: The politics of participatory democracy in Porto Alegre,* Stanford, CA: Stanford University Press.

Baiocchi, G., & Ganuza, E. (2012). The power of ambiguity: How participatory budgeting travels the globe. *Journal of Public Deliberation, 8*(2), article 8.

Baiocchi, G., & Ganuza, E. (2017). *Popular democracy: The paradox of participation.* Stanford, CA: Stanford University Press.

Bernhard, M., & O'Neill, D. (2018). The persistence of authoritarianism, *American Political Science Association, 16*(3), 595–598. doi: 10.1017/S1537592718001810

Blee, K., & Creasap, K. (2010). Conservative and right-wing movements. *Annual Review of Sociology, 36,* 269–286.

Bosman, J., Davey, M., & Smith, S. (2016, January 21). As water problems grew, officials belittled complaints from Flint. *The New York Times.* Retrieved from www.nytimes.com/2016/01/21/us/flint-michigan-lead-water-crisis.html?_r=0

Dewey, J. (1993). Philosophy and Democracy (1919). In D. Morris & I. Shapiro (Eds.), *John Dewey: The political writings* (pp. 38–47). Indianapolis, IN: Hackett Publishing Company.

Dewey, J. (2002). *Human nature and conduct* (2nd ed.). Toronto, Canada: General Publishing Company.

Drolet, J. (2010). Containing the Kantian revolutions: A theoretical analysis of the neoconservative critique of global liberal governance. *Review of International Studies, 36,* 533–560.

Drolet, J., & Williams, M. (2018). Radical conservatism and global order: International theory and the new right. *International Theory, 10*(3), 285–313.

Dryzek, J., Bächtiger, A., Chambers, S., Cohen, J., Druckman, J., Felicetti, A., ... Warren, M. (2019). The crisis of democracy and the science of deliberation: Citizens can avoid polarization and make sound decisions. *Science, 363*(6432), 1144–1146. doi: 10.1126/science aaw2694

Foa, R., & Mounk, Y. (2016). The danger of deconsolidation: The democratic discontent. *Journal of Democracy, 27*(3), 5–17.

Foa, R., & Mounk, Y. (2017). The signs of deconsolidation. *Journal of Democracy, 28*(1), 5–15.

Foster, J. (1981). The theory of institutional adjustment. *Journal of Economic Issues, 15*(4), 923–928.

Frank, T. (2005). *What's the matter with Kansas? How conservatives won the heart of America.* New York: Holt Paperbacks.

Galbraith, J. (2009). *The predator state: How conservatives abandoned the free market and why liberals should too* (2nd ed.). New York: Free Press.

Gogoi, P. (2019, January 21). Analysis: How the rise of the far right threatens democracy worldwide. Retrieved from www.npr.org/2019/01/21/687128474/analysis-how-the-rise-of-the-far-right-threatens-democracy-worldwide/

Golder, M. (2016). Far right parties in Europe. *Annual Review of Political Science, 19,* 477–497.

Greenberg, E. S. (1983). *The American political system* (3rd ed.). New York: Little, Brown & Company.

Heller, P. (2001). Moving the state: The politics of democratic decentralization in Kerala, South Africa, and Porto Alegre. *Politics of Society, 29*(1), 131–163.

Heller, P. (2009). Democratic deepening in India and South Africa. *Journal of Asian and African Studies, 44*(1), 123–149.

Heller, P., & Rao, V. (2015). Deliberation and development. In P. Heller & V. Rao (Eds.), *Deliberation and development: Rethinking the role of voice and collective action in unequal societies* (pp. 1–23). Washington, DC: World Bank Group.

Hobolt, S. (2016). The Brexit vote: A divided nation, a divided continent. *Journal of European Public Policy, 23*(9), 1259–1277.

Kossis, L. (2012). Examining the conflict between municipal receivership and local autonomy. *Virginia Law Review, 98*(5), 1109–1148.

Lerner, J. (2014). *Everyone counts: Could participatory budgeting change democracy?* Ithaca, NY: Cornell University Press.

Mansbridge, J. (2015). Minimalist definition of deliberation. In P. Heller & V. Rao (Eds.), *Deliberation and development: Rethinking the role of voice and collective action in unequal societies* (pp. 27–50). Washington, DC: World Bank Group.

Marquetti, A., da Silva, C. S., & Campbell, A. (2012). Participatory economic democracy in action: Participatory budgeting in Porto Alegre, 1989–2004. *Review of Radical Political Economics, 44*(1), 62–81.

Milner, H., & Katznelson, I. (2002). *Political science: State of the discipline.* New York: W. W. Norton & Company.

Norris, P., & Inglehart, R. (2019). *Cultural backlash: Trump, Brexit, and authoritarian populism.* New York: Cambridge University Press.

Putnam, R. (2000). *Bowling alone.* New York: Simon & Schuster Paperbacks.

Sen, A. (2001). *Development as freedom.* Oxford: Oxford University Press.

Siegel, S. (2017) Friend or foe? The LGBT community in the eyes of right-wing populism. *EuropeNow*, Retrieved from www.europenowjournal.org/2017/07/05/friend-or-foe-the-lgbt-community-in-the-eyes-of-right-wing-populism/

Sintomer, Y., Herzberg, C., Röcke, A., & Allegretti, G. (2012). Transnational models of citizen participation: The case of participatory budgeting. *Journal of Public Deliberation, 8*(2), article 9.

Skidmore, M. J. (1993). *Ideologies: Politics in action* (2nd ed.). San Diego, CA: Harcourt Brace Jovanovich College Publishers.

Talpin, J. (2011). *Schools of democracy.* London: European Consortium for Political Research.

Tool, M. (2000). *Value theory and economic progress: The institutional economics of J. Fagg Foster.* Boston, MA: Kluwer Academic Publishers.

Wampler, B. (2007a). *Participatory budgeting in Brazil: Contestation, cooperation, and accountability.* University Park, PA: The Pennsylvania State University Press.

Wampler, B. (2007b). A guide to participatory budgeting. In A. Shah (Ed.), *Participatory budgeting* (pp. 21–53). Washington, DC: The World Bank.

Whitman, W. (1982). *Whitman: Poetry and prose.* New York: The Library of America.

Williams, M. (2008). *The roots of participatory democracy: Democratic communists in South Africa and Kerala, India.* New York: Palgrave Macmillan.

2 Theoretical Framework

This is primarily an emergent philosophical study of PB. It is a philosophical study because it uses historical ideas developed prior to the invention of PB, pertaining to the potential benefits of PB. It is emergent in the sense that PB is an emerging phenomenon that is constantly changing and evolving due to the changing political and economic dynamics affecting each individual PB process. These potential benefits are social phenomena, which are the result of historical processes moving through time within specific cultural contexts. "Every social phenomenon, however, is itself a sequential course of changes, and hence a fact isolated from the history of which it is a moving constituent loses the qualities that make it distinctively social" (Dewey, 1938, p. 501). This is one reason why it is helpful to do a philosophical study that examines the history of these social phenomena.

By studying the philosophies of PB's potential benefits, we can better comprehend how they occur and better perceive their effect on individuals and society. An awareness of the relevant philosophies is needed in order to better understand the potential benefits of PB so that recommendations can be made which will permit PB's potential benefits to be realized. Broadly speaking, the effect PB has on the Political Economy is examined.

In this case, Political Economy is used in the classical sense. The classical economists considered areas outside the scope of current orthodox economics, such as social, political, and historical processes (Forstater, 2004). Institutional Economics is used to analyze the problem and determine a course of action. As mentioned in Chapter 1, Institutional Economics is one field of study within heterodox economics, which means it is not part of orthodox economics. PB's potential effects on politics are explored by reviewing the relevant writings of Thomas Jefferson, John Dewey, and others. By using the Political Economy methodology, this study explores all the effects PB has on society. "Political economy considers society as a whole; ethical values are prominent and are embodied in specific institutions, and historical considerations are important" (Bortis, 1999, 17). The ethical implications of PB are examined in the relevant writings of Alfred Schutz and others. Thus, Political Economy, in this sense, perceives that various aspects of society are related to, and influence, one another.

Theoretical Framework 27

Doing this research necessitates an interdisciplinary approach. The study of local governance is part of Political Science. Sociology includes the study of human social relationships. And Economics is about the provisioning of society. Although, social provisioning would be more about heterodox economics than orthodox economics. And of course, Institutional Economics is part of heterodox economics. The social issues in today's world are complex and interrelated and do not fit neatly into the fields of study as defined by academia.

The hypothesis of this research monograph is that as PB processes become more deliberative, more empowered, and greatly expanded the more participants will experience public happiness, greater understanding of others, greater development of morality, and an increased sense of belonging. And it is proposed that PB processes be expanded until they are making all, or most, local decisions. It is difficult to prove that a social innovation such as local direct democracies will result in the benefits described in the hypothesis. However, the philosophical research in this study proves that the hypothesis is possible in the following four ways.

First, examples are provided to illustrate that the independent variables in the hypothesis and the direct action needed to realize them have, in the past, been successfully implemented. The independent variables include successful empowered PB processes, a successful deliberative society, and direct action resulting in substantial improvement of social justice issues. The initial PB process in Porto Alegre was designed such that other municipal bureaucratic agencies were below PB in the administrative hierarchy, which empowered their PB process (Chapter 1) and is one reason the PB process in Porto Alegre was designated a best practice at the United Nations Habitat II meeting in Istanbul in 1996 (Goldfrank, 2012). An example of a deliberative society, which was successful for hundreds of years, was the League of the Iroquois (Chapter 7) around the time the first settlers came to the New England area of America. In the 1960s, students, and others, proved that direct action could, and did, result in substantial improvement of social justice issues. In America, the SDS (Students for a Democratic Society) engaged in direct action (Chapter 6), which helped several social movements.

Second, a chapter is devoted to each of the four potential benefits of PB (Chapters 4 to 7). Social philosophers are quoted in each chapter to provide insight of each social phenomenon in order to better understand the importance of each and how each might be realized. This provides reasonable certainty that these benefits will result from the implementation of the independent variables.

Third, other research has been referenced in Chapter 3 that shows what needs to be done in order to create quality public deliberation and an infrastructure to support the direct action needed to empower and expand PBNYC (PB in New York City), which is proposed as the initial site for this proposed social innovation. In Chapter 3 the conditions needed for public deliberation are reviewed and specific recommendations are made to improve and monitor public deliberation. The need to fund and coordinate a city-wide campaign of direct action to further empower and expand the scope of responsibilities for PBNYC is also discussed in Chapter 3.

28   *Theoretical Framework*

Finally, and perhaps the most important contribution of the social philosophers, is the vision they provide of a better life. Throughout this research the social philosophers paint a realistic picture of the possibility of people working together in their communities and having a sense of belonging to their communities. Building the community by working with everyone in the community will improve the quality of life in the community and build the character of the individuals doing the work. This is the motivation people need in order to devote their time and energy to the cause of revitalizing democracy. Thus, the people will prove this hypothesis true by living it.

The first section defines and reviews the scope of social provisioning as it pertains to this study. The second section examines how Institutional Economics is used in this research. First the work of Dewey concerning how science can be used in social research is reviewed. Then the work of Foster is examined to see how his instrumental theory of value and his theory of institutional adjustment apply to this study. His theory of institutional adjustment is used to identify an adjustment that should be made in the PB process. The interface between PB and city agencies should change. Specifically, allowing bureaucratic agencies within city government to arbitrarily change or ignore PB decisions based on the agencies' internal priorities or biases detracts from the instrumental value of the PB process. The final section is about the social philosophers and further explains why the philosophical approach is the best approach to evaluate the hypothesis of this research.

Social Provisioning

This study is an investigation into the ways that the PB process affects the social provisioning process. Since human beings are social beings, relationships are what most matter. They are what give meaning and purpose to life. Economics should not be solely concerned with the provisioning of our physical needs.

Power, a feminist economist, gives the following definition of social provisioning.

> "Social provisioning" is a phrase that draws attention away from images of pecuniary [money] pursuits and individual competition, and toward notions of sustenance, cooperation, and support. ... Social provisioning need not be done through the market; it need not be done for selfish or self-interested reasons, although neither of these is inconsistent with social provisioning either. Thus, the concept allows for a broader understanding of economic activity.
>
> (Power, 2004, p. 6)

Social provisioning enables one to look in a more holistic way at economics and its interaction with society. Lee's entry in *The New Palgrave Dictionary of Economics* defines heterodox economics in terms of social provisioning.

Theoretical Framework 29

[H]eterodox economists extend their theory to examining issues associated with the process of social provisioning, such as racism, gender and ideologies and myths. Because their economics involves issues of ethical values and social philosophy and the historic aspects of human existence, heterodox economists make ethically based *economic policy* recommendations to improve human dignity, that is, recommending ameliorative and/or radical, social and economic policies to improve the social provisioning and hence well-being for all members of society and especially the disadvantaged members.

(2008, p.4)

In this study, the social provisioning process refers to all the relationships, organizations, and customs that go toward the production and distribution of all the goods and services that are used to satisfy human needs, including the fundamental tangible needs, such as food, clothing, and shelter, as well as intangible needs. These needs may or may not be exchanged through the market (Dugger, 1996; Power, 2004). This study includes a comprehensive review of the ways PB's intangible benefits, as defined in this research, affects society and the economy, from a social provisioning perspective. This includes how the quality of community decision-making for political and economic issues effects the well-being of individual participants and their communities.

Since people are social beings, the provisioning process should address our social needs as well as our physical needs. Alternative economic theories to the neoclassical, or orthodox, view, while in the classical tradition,

see the economic problem to be both physical and social. The physical problem of economics is to make sure that the productive system, particularly that portion which serves human *needs*, can be maintained and can produce a surplus. The social problem is that of designing appropriate institutions which can cultivate the *higher* needs of human society while at the same time providing for society's subsistence needs.

(Lichtenstein, 1983, p. xiii)

PB is an institution that can address both types of needs. It allocates public goods and services, as authorized by the city. PB is also able to address some higher needs of human society. Well-designed PB processes allow people to develop as individuals when they engage others in public forums and make decisions. The local direct democracies resulting from expanding PB processes would also address both types of needs. Of course, the communities also benefit from people coming together to help one another.

Institutional Economics

The foundation of Institutional Economics is based on the writings of Thorstein Veblen. Institution Economics is based on the Veblenian dichotomy

30 *Theoretical Framework*

which analyzes our patterns of behavior, thought, and valuing (Sturgeon, 2010). The dichotomy consists of the institutional and the technological (Foster, 1981a). Institutions are habits of thought and behavior that come from myths, legends, and traditions. Institutions are social traditions and beliefs that are passed from generation to generation. The Institutional part of the dichotomy is resistant to change. Technology refers to learned behaviors and patterns of thought associated with the machine process and the scientific method. The machine process dictates the most efficient way to use tools. Technology means behavior that is instrumentally verifiable. But it is not just about using tools; it is about approaching life with a scientific curiosity and gaining knowledge. Technology is the dynamic side of the dichotomy that promotes change. Veblen believed that change is the result of a scientific curiosity. This curiosity leads mankind to investigate everything using the scientific methodology, which results in new scientifically verified knowledge. New knowledge about new ways of doing things conflicts with traditional beliefs. Positive change occurs when scientifically verified knowledge is used in place of tradition beliefs.

Dewey's Scientific Method

Dewey believed that social inquiry, as well as the physical sciences, could use the scientific method to guide research. There are additional challenges in the social sciences to using the scientific method. "One obvious source of the difficulty lies in the fact that the subject-matter of the later [social inquiry] is so "complex" and so intricately interwoven that the difficulty of instituting a relatively closed system...is intensified" (Dewey, 1938, p. 487). It is not really possible to isolate a particular social interaction from other social interactions. "All inquiry proceeds within a cultural matrix which is ultimately determined by the nature of social relations" (Dewey, 1938, p. 487). Thus, in social inquiry, it is harder to prove cause and effect.

This is why all the effects of social policy need to be closely monitored. Then the results of monitoring need to be used to refine the public policy in question.

> Dewey's "method of intelligence" aims at making indeterminate situations into determinate ones: his vision of the method of science thus focuses on social control through democratic institutions. An integral part of this process is making self-adjusting or self-correcting value judgements in addressing problematic situations. This is not only the essence of scientific method as it is practiced in experimental laboratories by chemists and physicists, according to Dewey, it is also the method of democracy or, at least, it is most compatible with democratic institutions.
>
> (Tillman, 1987, p. 1387)

The scientific methodology would seem to be compatible with and useful for democratic governance.

Theoretical Framework 31

The first step is to define the problem statement. Dewey wrote, "the ultimate end and test of all inquiry is the transformation of a problematic situation (which involves confusion and conflict) into a unified one" (1938, p. 491). As was stated previously, there are dozens, if not hundreds, of different implementations of PB around the world. These differences are due to different rules, procedures, and practices for the various PB processes. Of course, these differences produce a corresponding number of effects on PB's potential benefits. There seems to be some confusion concerning what the practical goals of PB should be or could be.

Concerning Dewey's view of the problem statement.

> It is commonly assumed that the problems which exist are already definite in their main features. When this assumption is made, it follows that the business of inquiry is but to ascertain the best method of solving them. The consequence of this assumption is that the work of analytic discrimination, which is necessary to convert a problematic situation into a set of conditions forming a definite problem, is largely foregone.
>
> (1938, p. 495)

A problem must be studied before proceeding to the next step. Dewey's solution is straightforward. "The lesson, as far as method of social inquiry is concerned, is the prime necessity for development of techniques of analytic observation and comparison, so that problematic social situations may be resolved into definitely formulated problems" (Dewey, 1938, p. 494).[1] The careful study of the problematic social situation is needed to reveal the "facts."

Dewey proposed a scientific methodology for social inquiry that is used in this study to gain a better understanding of how to adjust the PB process. Dewey wrote, "facts have to be determined in their dual function as obstacles and as resources" (1938, p. 499). The dual function of facts is related to the social phenomenon being studied. Facts can either impede the movement toward a social phenomenon or facts can help a desired social phenomenon occur. For PB, the facts are the rules, procedures, and practices of each PB process.

The rules of PB include what types of projects PB may consider, amounts of money available, who is eligible to participate in PB, and the timing of the annual budget cycle. Enough money needs to be available for projects that are important to people in order to help get them excited about participating. The procedures of PB include the seating arrangement of participants and the use of facilitators. Procedures can either encourage or discourage deliberation. Practices in the PB process may include how PB reaches out to traditionally disenfranchised groups within the community as well as inviting specific individuals to neighborhood assemblies in order to encourage deliberation.

It is important to understand how the facts of this study relate to the social phenomena being studied. For example, when the rules, procedures, and practices of PB empower participants to make decisions affecting their community, the participants can experience a sense of belonging. Also, when participants

32   *Theoretical Framework*

publicly deliberate, they can gain a better understanding of each other. These relationships are explored in the following chapters.

In Chapter 3, specific rules, practices, and procedures are proposed that should result in the desired social phenomena. Additionally, later in this chapter Foster's theory of institutional adjustment is used to identify an adjustment which will make PB more instrumentally effective. In this study, the desired social phenomena are the potential benefits of PB which include increasing public happiness, becoming more understanding of others, strengthening a sense of belonging, and developing our morality. These social phenomena are intertwined and tend to reinforce each other.

Scientific methodology requires that the results of any experiment be examined. Dewey wrote:

> that policies and proposals for social action be treated as working hypothesis, not as programs to be rigidly adhered to and executed. They will be experimental in the sense that they will be entertained subject to constant and well-equipped observation of the consequences they entail when acted upon, and subject to ready and flexible revision in the light of observed consequences.
>
> (1954, pp. 202–203)

It should be expected that changes may need to be made in the light of observed consequences. And even if things are going as expected for a period of time, changing political and economic forces may affect the PB processes in unexpected ways.

For social inquiry, it is important to keep in mind Dewey's means-end-continuum. The means-end-continuum refers to the fact that ends are the means to future ends; and, means are the ends of prior actions. Thus, they both have consequences. Sometimes the consequences are unintended.

> The sole alternative to the view that *the* end is an arbitrarily selected part of actual consequences which as "the end" then justifies the use of means irrespective of the other consequences they produce, is that desires, ends-in-view, and consequences achieved be valued in turn as means of further consequences.
>
> (Dewey, 1972, p. 42)

The end does not justify the means. Any additional consequences of the means, as well as consequences of the end should be continuously evaluated so that decisions can be made concerning possible future adjustment of the means used or possible future adjustment of the originally proposed end. It should be anticipated that adjustments will need to be made to PB processes.

It is important to continuously monitor projects and programs approved by PB to ensure that their original goals are being met. It is also important to monitor for unintended consequences. Human society is complex and dynamic.

Theoretical Framework   33

Foster's Theories

Foster published very little; instead, he chose to focus on passing knowledge on to his students in the classroom, as part of the oral tradition. In 1981, the *Journal of Economic Issues* published several of his previously unpublished papers, with introductory passages written by Baldwin Ranson.

Foster's theory of institutional adjustment was part of his search for the unification of the concepts of economics (Foster, 1981a). His theory of institutional adjustment is based on his instrumental theory of value. In the introduction to "The Theory of Institutional Adjustment," Ranson wrote,

> Unification was necessary and could be approached, Foster maintained, through the theory of institutional adjustment. Such a theory is a particular application of a unified theory of value, which in turn is a particular application of the theory of knowledge on which science must be erected.
>
> (Foster, 1981a, p. 923)

Foster refined the Veblenian dichotomy to ceremonial behavior – instrumental behavior. This helped, because for many people technology was all about tools and their use. Using instrumental behavior in place of technology emphasized that the process was more than just about tools. Instrumental behavior is about promoting the life process (Tool, 2000) and using the scientific method to guide your behavior. It is about intelligent behavior. And replacing institutional behavior with ceremonial behavior was helpful because people confused institutions with organizations. Ceremonial behavior is about using myths, legends, and traditions to guide your behavior. "Foster's ceremonial-instrumental dichotomy is such a significant refinement of the institution-technology dichotomy that it can be considered qualitatively different" (Waller, 1982, p. 764). Clarifying the terminology made the dichotomy more useful in analyzing human behavior.

The dichotomy helps us to understand and explain change. One of the few constants in modern life is change. Change is driven by the instrumental behavior of constantly seeking and applying new knowledge, which causes stress because it is met with resistance from ceremonial behavior. This stress is relived when change occurs. "For behavior to change a break or adjustment in ceremonial values is required" (Sturgeon, 2010, p. 17). Human behavior can be broken down and examined by using the dichotomy (Sturgeon, 2010).

To understand human behavior one must understand philosophy as well as science. "Foster argues that science and philosophy ... cover the same areas, they explain the same things in the same fashion" (Tool, 2000, p. 13). Philosophy is normative and science is substantive. However, value is used as the criteria of judgment, which is used to make choices. How can choices be made without a normative component? Judgment links "what is" (substantive) to "what ought to be" (normative) (Tool, 2000). "Judgement is the connecting link between the present and the future [Foster 1950(LN) Value, 2]" (Tool, 2000, p. 78). Analysis must proceed on this basis because "[T]he concept of value

34 *Theoretical Framework*

must be in terms of process because the *whole* of our experience has been with process ... [T]o be a true concept, it must display the attribute we call continuity [Foster 1950 (LN) Value, 2 (emphasis in original)]" (Tool, 2000, p. 78). Value must be in terms of the social process (Tool, 2000).

Foster's instrumental theory of value is based on the ceremonial behavior – instrumental behavior dichotomy. "*Value theory identifies and explains criteria of judgement*" (Tool, 2000, p. 36). His theory of value defines instrumental behavior to include that which promotes the life process, as explained by Ranson, a student of Foster's.

> To apply the Veblenian distinction, ask of any object of inquiry: What elements promote the life process? What elements obstruct the life process? The first elements are called instrumental, developmental, serviceable, and/ or productive. The second elements are called ceremonial, acquisitive, invidious, and/or wasteful (Ranson 1999).
>
> (Tool, 2000, p. 75)

Promoting the life process is logically necessary, which is clearly an instrumental behavior. To judge whether something promotes the life process one must look at human experiences and the community as a whole. "The continuing existential universe in which value theory is developed and utilized is perceived by Foster to be the encompassing social process. This social process is the locus of Foster's value theory" (Tool, 2000, p. 68). Thus, instrumental value theory is grounded in reality.

The question remains as to whether other criteria of judgment such as moral or ethical should be used in some circumstances in place of the instrumental criteria. From a paper presented to the 2008 meeting of the Association for Evolutionary Economics, we learn the following:

> Some philosophers (e.g. Habermas, 9) add to Foster's instrumental criterion an ethical and a moral criterion, dividing "what ought-to-be into three distinct species: pragmatic [the instrumental], ethical [the good], and moral [the just]. But this division denies the unity and continuity of human experience. Foster insisted that these three names all refer to a single trait of desirability: continuity. What ought-to-be because it achieves continuity is the same as what ought-to-be morally and ethically – the position adopted by "deep ecology" (Capra, 7, 11, 297).
>
> (Ranson, 2008)

Foster did not see a distinction between instrumental criteria and ethical or moral criteria. It makes sense for everyone, including the deep ecology movement, to place a high value on the attribute of continuity.

Concerning the community's well-being, Foster believed that democratic decision-making was instrumental. "As Foster continuously reminded his students, *democracy*, because of its continuous promotion of reasoned discourse and instrumental design, *is the most instrumentally efficient approach to social policy-making known*" (Tool, 2000, p. 103).

Foster's theory of institutional adjustment is based on his theory of value. "Institutional change takes the form of a change in the value structure of the institution" (Bush, 1988, p. 149). Values are the basis of judgment concerning choices. "The embedding of Foster's instrumental value theory in his theory of institutional adjustment permits the joining of normative and substantive elements for guidance in problem solving" (Tool, 2000, p. 89). Normative judgments can be a guide for problem solving by being used to further the life process and the well-being of the community.

No cookie-cutter solutions for institutional problems are provided.

> Foster's instrumental value theory addresses degrees and/or levels of instrumentalness in appraising institutional structure. It has no directional constant in the sense of installing and/or implementing otherwise warranted (ceremonial, invidious, coercive) institutional adjustments. It has no teleological "drivers" (e.g. natural laws) that inherently shape the direction and implementation of institutional adjustments. It offers no ideological institutional recipes – capitalism, communism, fascism – to serve as all-purpose, all encompassing, institutional solutions for problems confronted.
>
> (Tool, 2000, p. 81)

Foster's instrumental value theory simply promotes the life process.

In the introduction to Foster's "The Theory of Institutional Adjustment," Ranson wrote, "Foster considers a real economic problem to exist whenever there is disrapport [disharmony] among human activities that are supposed to be correlated in continuance of the productive process" (Foster, 1981a, p. 924). It is important to know what is meant by correlated behavior.

> The term "patterns of correlated behavior" embodies two important concepts: (1) the notion that behavior within an institution is not random but purposeful and correlated; and (2) the notion that "values" function as the "correlators" of behavior within and among patterns of behavior.
>
> (Bush, 1988, p. 127)

Foster's theory of value is how behavior is correlated to promote the life process. "Values function as the standards of judgement by which behavior is correlated" (Bush, 1988, p. 127). This is significant because as Tool wrote, "Foster's instrumental value theory is grounded in existential and experiential phenomena, evidentially affirmed" (2000, p. 82). Thus, judgment is based on relevant criteria.

Within Foster's definition of an economic problem, replacing "productive process" with "social provisioning process," as previously defined, would make this definition of a real economic problem inclusive of all economic activity and applicable to the scope of this study. If there is any disharmony within PB

36 Theoretical Framework

processes that should be correlated in continuance of the social provisioning process, a real economic problem exists.

The problem statement is how can the potential benefits of PB, for both individuals and communities, in addition to the provisioning of public goods and services, be realized? The hypothesis of this study is that as PB processes become more deliberative, more empowered, and greatly expanded the more participants will experience public happiness, greater understanding of others, greater development of morality, and an increased sense of belonging.

Foster introduced the concept of institutional adjustment as an alternative to the concept of institutional evolution. His theory of institutional adjustment consists of three principles.

> These three principles are altogether different than what is presented in standard textbooks as the principles of economics. But if economics is a social science (and it certainly is) and if social science is to maintain significance in the sense of being applicable to real problems, and if answers to all social problems necessarily take the form of institutional adjustments (which they appear to do) then the principles of economics will have to be conceived and stated in such terms [(1972) 1981, 942].
>
> (Tool, 2000, p. 87)

After the three principles of institutional adjustment are met, adjustment takes place.

Foster developed his theory of institutional adjustment in order to evaluate and improve the productive process of institutions. I use it a slightly different way. The institution under review is PB, which is an institution solely dedicated to reviving the idea, and the ideal, of democracy, which Foster believed "*is the most instrumentally efficient approach to policy making known*" (Tool, 2000, p. 103), as noted earlier. Thus, any contributions a PB process makes to the social provisioning process would include some, or all, of the intangible benefits of people participating in local direct democracy.

The first principle is instrumental primacy (Sturgeon, 2010, p. 48).[2] Before any institutional adjustment can take place there must be some stress within the institution's value structure. This stress increases over time when the instrumental experience of value increasingly differs from the ceremonial set of values. Part of this principle is recognizing the difference between "what is being done" and "what ought to be done" (Foster, 1981b). In the case of PB, it is clear that better results for individual participants and the community could be achieved. For example, if PB has more funding they could do more outreach, hire more translators, and do more training.

The second principle is recognized interdependence (Foster, 1981b). Members in the institution who will be affected must recognize how their relationships will be modified, and they need to accept the new pattern. This principle identifies what is needed to get from "what is" to "what ought to be" (Foster, 1981b). This may be the most important principle for the PB process.

Once people recognize that they are part of a community, they should be more willing to take an active role in the PB process. "The principle of recognized interdependence is simply that the immediate pattern of any institutional adjustment is specified by the pattern of interdependencies recognized by the members of the institution" (Foster, 1981b, p. 933). In the case of PB, this means that people recognize their interdependence with others in the community. They see themselves as part of the community. As participation in PB increases, due to changes outlined in the next chapter, participants should increasingly recognize their interdependence with other PB participants and other civic groups as they work to improve their community.

The third principle is minimal dislocation (Foster, 1981b). "Minimal Dislocation deals with the circumstance that adjustments must actually be capable of integration into the remainder of the existing social fabric" (Sturgeon, 2010, p. 9). This includes the situation where adjustments made in one institution may cause related adjustments to occur in other institutions. In this circumstance, this principle states that changes required of another institution cannot be greater than that institution is able to do. This principle is about the limits to the extent or speed of an adjustment (Foster, 1981b). For PBNYC (PB in NYC), this refers to the city agencies that must approve and implement PBNYC decisions.

The three principles are necessary and sufficient to explain the process of institutional adjustment. They address what is needed for an institution to perceive that an adjustment is needed, how the members of the institution need to respond, as well as defining the limitations of the adjustment. Once each PB process is able to satisfy these principles, PB should be able to realize its potential benefits.

Before a social inquiry about the PB process can proceed, a specific PB process must be selected. Because, as noted earlier, almost every PB process is different from almost every other one. I choose PBNYC to test whether the transformative potential of PB can be realized, because as Su wrote, "Participatory budgeting in New York City (PBNYC), for both its magnitude and its potential as a model to be copied, has become a decisive case to critically examine" (2017, p. 68).

During investigation of PBNYC, a situation was found relating to the third principle of minimal dislocation. The municipal agencies responsible for approving and implementing decisions made by PBNYC apparently have not been able to change to be able to efficiently work with PBNYC.

The relationship between PB and the city agencies is critical to the success of PBNYC. For example, city agencies determine which projects are feasible.

> [T]he facially neutral criteria of feasibility quickly took precedence over community need and priority, and sidelined the sorts of testimony and evidence – based on lived experiences on which neighborhood areas felt less safe at night, or which schools required dire repairs, for instance – more likely to be put forward by traditionally marginalized constituents. Instead, the constituents most likely to forward successful projects were those who

38   *Theoretical Framework*

tailored (or even created) their projects to fit city agencies' PB project criteria. [From an interview with a former facilitator on 10/21/2015] "I ended up dropping out of PB ... I was so disgusted with ... [projects] ... being contorted to look like – to be defined as – need for technology" ... These criteria are thus best and most easily manipulated by those with legal and bureaucratic connections, skills in logic and discursive framing, and grant proposal-writing skills to "distort" their desires into PB-eligible "needs."

(Su, 2017, p. 134)

Thus, large portions of the community without such knowledge of the bureaucracies are essentially left out of the process.

The exclusionary effect of city agencies' criteria for PB projects was apparent in where the winning project proposals originated.

For example, in the first PB cycle in 2011–2012, ideas submitted through the online platform constituted twenty percent of all ideas proposed in district 39; yet, more than half of winning projects originated in the online platform. By contrast, most of that districts' neighborhood assemblies (where face-to-face deliberation took place) did not yield any winning projects that year, despite high and active participation. This fits well with findings that city-wide, the PB online platform most engaged white, well-educated, and higher-income constituents.

(Su, 2017, p. 135)

This has a discriminatory effect on which proposals are approved by city agencies.

Apparently, even after a proposal went through a neighborhood assembly and was agreeable to the budget committee, the project idea could be overruled by a city agency.

Budget delegates complained that their original project ideas, which spoke to dire community needs, were often sidelined and replaced by questionably needed projects that appeared easy to implement. Predictably, these projects were also those prioritized by city agencies or championed by already powerful groups.

(Su, 2017, p. 135)

Thus, the interface between PBNYC and the city agencies that approve and implement PBNYC decisions will need to be changed to allow for a rapid increase in the size of PBNYC as well as a substantial increase in the types of projects and programs that PBNYC will be allowed to decide. Chapter 3 has a recommendation that will remove this bottleneck in PBNYC decisions. Also addressed is a recommendation of how this change can be implemented. Additionally, Chapter 3 has several other recommendations. However, the added recommendations do not involve structural adjustments, just the need for funding, which is also addressed in Chapter 3.

Theoretical Framework 39

One more insight about social inquiry that recommends change. People will be motivated once they see that the potential rewards are worth the effort. This is where the social philosophers can create a vision of a better life working toward the democratic ideal. People need to envisage the potential benefits, which include increasing feelings of public happiness, gaining better understanding of others, helping to develop individual and community morality, and gaining a sense of belonging.

> "People will accept physical changes ... without requiring to know how it works or why its result is produced" (879). Not so with social inquiry; a "condition of application is understanding by the persons involved ... [T]he results of social inquiry cannot be accomplished in any large measure without the results themselves being a part of peoples' knowledge, and that knowledge must be operational ... (879).
>
> (Tool, 2000, p. 18)

The need for people to understand the potential benefits of this social inquiry is further addressed in the next section about social philosophers.

Social Philosophers

Why use philosophical research for this study? Democracy is really about morality because equality is a key concept of democracy, which demands that everyone is treated with dignity and respect. Democracy is an ideal of a better way of life. John Dewey was a social philosopher who addressed the question of why philosophy is the best avenue to advocate for a better way of life.

> [H]e [John Dewey] never abandons his earliest conception of philosophy as a vehicle for clarifying a society's dominate interest, for speaking "the authentic idiom [expression] of an enduring and dominating corporate [unified body of individuals] experience." In other words, philosophy expresses not "truth," but as its etymology suggests, "wisdom" – "a sense for the better kind of life to be led." "Meaning," Dewey contends, "is wider in scope as well as more precious in value than is truth, and philosophy is occupied with meaning rather than with truth."
>
> (Morris & Shapiro, 1993, p. xv–xvi)

This research is about transforming an exciting and successful social innovation, PB, into something bigger and even more transformative. It is about a new and better way of life.

Philosophy can help people choose a way of life they have not yet experienced because philosophy can be defined as a love of wisdom.

> Wisdom is a moral term ... As a moral term it refers to a choice about something to be done, a preference for living this sort of life rather than that. It

40   *Theoretical Framework*

refers not to accomplished reality but to a desired future which our desires, when translated into articulate conviction, may help bring into existence.

(Dewey, 1993a, p. 39)

One way to look at this study is that it explores one way for people to develop their morality (Chapter 6), which will be reflected not only in their local governments but in the state and federal governments as well. "Governments have their origin in the moral identity of men" (Emerson, 1983, p. 566). The morality of men expresses itself in their governments. As individuals develop their morality, they will vote for individuals that reflect their morality.

And of course, social philosophers are very good at defining and explaining social interaction. Social interaction is how individuals develop their potential. "He [Dewey] argues that liberalism's original and justly enduring values such as autonomy and self-realization are best served now...by organization and 'social action': thinking, working, and pursuing our social and political ideals together" (Morris & Shapiro, 1993, p. xiii). Working together is how we work on improving ourselves.

The development of the individual is the solution to the ethical problem of the relationship of the individual to the state (Dewey, 1993b). "Such a development of the individual [realization of capacities] that he shall be in harmony with all others in the state, that is, that he shall possess as his own the unified will of the community" (Dewey, 1993b, p. 59). Public communication serves the dual purpose of helping individuals as well as helping the community. There is no real conflict between individuals' interests and communities' interests.

Another reason to study historical social philosophers is that sometimes their literature can influence people more than other methods. "The art of literature catches men unaware and employs a charm to bring them to a spot whence they see vividly and intimately some picture which embodies life in a meaning" (Dewey, 1993a, p. 40). Perhaps this approach will allow us to put aside partisan positions and allow us to objectivity consider what is best for us and future generations.

Three of the social philosophers reviewed in this research are Transcendentalists. They are Ralph Waldo Emerson, Henry David Thoreau, and Walt Whitman. They were a group of American writers and poets from the mid-nineteenth century who believed that people should follow their conscience, "The transcendentalists did not rely solely upon reason. The emphasis instead was upon a consciousness of the absolute, the result more of intuition than of reason" (Skidmore, 1998, p. 143). The Transcendentalists believed that consciousness could reveal wisdom. They believed that God is within each of us, which is why they believed that self-reflection is the key to self-improvement.

Emerson wrote about the capacity of people. This would include the capacity of people to govern themselves. Emerson tried to inspire people with his writings and speeches. A specific example of Emerson's work intended to inspire was *Representative Men*, in which he wrote about six people whom he considered to be "great men." They were persons who might motivate others to try to become heroes or geniuses. "All men were partial men, facets of perfect men. When anyone surrendered to himself, when he reflected his unique share of divinity, he was a hero, but not a perfect one" (Conkin, 1968, p. 167). Emerson believed that all men should aspire to be better because he believed that all men could better themselves by looking inward and reflecting on truth. "Emerson was recommending not that we worship or pattern ourselves on his subjects but that we use them as mirrors to take a new look at ourselves" (Ikeda, as cited in Bosco et al., 2009, p. 111). He believed that greatness is within each person. "The young man reveres men of genius, because, to speak truly, they are more himself than he is" (Emerson, 1983, p. 448). Emerson not only hoped to inspire people to achieve their full potential, but was confident that it was feasible.

Thoreau provides the philosophical and moral foundation for local direct democracy. Thoreau's views about government seem to be a paradox. He seems to favor democracy and yet he advocates that people everywhere follow their conscience. He definitely does not favor having no government. "But, to speak practically and as a citizen, unlike those who call themselves no-government men, I ask for, not at once no government, but at once a better government" (Thoreau, 1996, p. 2). Thoreau did see the need for government.

To a certain extent, Thoreau actually did appreciate the United States political system.

> Seen from a lower point of view, the Constitution, with all its faults, is very good; the law and the courts are very respectable; even this State and the American government are, in many respects, very admirable and rare things, to be thankful for ... but seen from a point of view a little higher, they are what I have described them; seen from a higher still, and the highest, who shall say what they are, or that they are worth looking at or thinking of at all?
>
> (Thoreau, 1996, p. 18)

Thoreau appreciated that Constitutional representative government was a tremendous improvement over earlier forms of government. However, he also could see the need for improvement of representative democracy.

He was concerned that representative government did not represent the best qualities of human nature. "We talk about a *representative* government; but what a monster of a government is that where the noblest faculties of the mind, and *whole* heart, are not *represented*" (Thoreau, 1996, p. 150). It seems Thoreau believed that an improved government would not be a government of elected representatives.

It would seem that a regional or local government by consensus might meet Thoreau's expectations. "The rights of the individual are paramount to Thoreau, and the only government he could respect would be one that comes about naturally through a consensus of conscience-driven individuals" (McIntyre, 2008, p. 8). Government by consensus would not be possible for large numbers of people. However, as discussed in Chapter 7, the Iroquois Confederacy was able

42   Theoretical Framework

to govern by consensus by using small political units (tribes). Some have said that Thoreau's political ideas require decentralization into small political units (Jenco, 2003; McWilliams, 1974). Local direct democracies where decisions are made by a consensus, or near consensus, of the community might meet Thoreau's expectations. Thus, in Thoreau's writings there seems to be the philosophical and moral justification for local direct democracies.

Walt Whitman was a Transcendentalist who believed that democracy was evolving. He provides a vision of what will happen. Whitman saw the democracy in the United States as proceeding in stages, with each stage building on the previous stage(s). "The first stage was the planning and putting on record the political foundation rights of immense masses of people" (Whitman, 1982, p. 976). This stage included the Declaration of Independence, the Constitution and its amendments, and the provisions for increased suffrage (Whitman, 1982). "The second stage relates to material prosperity, wealth, produce, labor-saving machines" (Whitman, 1982, p. 977). The second stage had arrived by the time of Whitman's work.

The third stage of democracy is what Whitman said is needed to support and encourage the American spirit.[3]

> The third stage, rising out of the previous ones, to make them and all illustrious, I, now, for one, promulge, announcing a native-spirit, getting into form, adult, and through mentality, for these States, self-contain'd, different from others, more expansive, more rich and free, to be evidenced by original authors and poets to come, by American personalities, plenty of them, male and female, traversing the States, none excepted – and by native superber tableaux and growths of language, songs, operas, orations, lectures, architecture – and by a sublime serious Religious Democracy sternly taking command, dissolving the old, sloughing off surfaces, and from its own interior and vital principles, reconstructing, democratizing society.
>
> (Whitman, 1982, p. 977)

Whitman saw the need to go beyond a democratic government toward a democratic society. Perhaps his reference in the quote to a sublime serious Religious Democracy can best be explained by the following quote from "Democratic Vistas":

> The climax of this loftiest range of civilization ... is to be its development from the eternal bases, and the fit expression, of absolute Conscience, moral soundness, Justice. Even in religious fervor there is a touch of animal heat. But moral conscientiousness, crystalline, without flaw, not Godlike only, entirely human, awes and enchants forever.
>
> (Whitman, 1982, p. 982)

Whitman believed that a democratic society is possible when society's moral conscientiousness reaches its zenith in a mix of religious fervor with a little animal heat. A very passionate deeply felt understanding of how to change things for the better can in fact change things for the better.

The next stage of democracy is a democratic society. Perhaps the first step toward the next stage is the formation of local direct democracies. Whitman affirms that this is a moral undertaking like no other. And that it will be driven by a passion unlike any other.

Finally, the last answer to the question of why use philosophical research for this study, is that social philosophers can tell us what we have been doing wrong. Dewey wrote in "Creative Democracy – The Task Before Us" that "we acted as if our democracy were something that perpetuated itself automatically; as if our ancestors had succeeded in setting up a machine that solved the problem of perpetual motion in politics" (1993c, p. 241). It takes more than voting every two years or every four years to ensure that democracy lives up to its potential.

Dewey wrote that democracy requires more from its citizens. It requires an ongoing active interest.

> I am inclined to believe that the heart and final guarantee of democracy is in free gatherings of neighbors on the street corner to discuss back and forth what is read in uncensored news of the day, and in gatherings of friends in the living rooms of houses and apartments to converse freely and with one another.
>
> (1993c, p. 243)

Ongoing discussions and deliberations within the community are a necessity and constitute part of Dewey's "proper conditions" for democracy to flourish.

Notes

1 This study relies on the ethnographic research in *Schools of Democracy*, a case study of PBNYC, and Foster's theory of institutional adjustment.
2 Foster's term was technological determinism. In Sturgeon's 2010 paper, he renamed it instrumental primacy. "The latter [instrumental primacy] is more in line with terminology used to define the Veblenian dichotomy and in light of contemporary usage of technological determinism, is less likely to be misunderstood."
3 Perhaps Whitman's idea of American spirit could be equated with Jefferson's idea of public happiness (see Chapter 4), which he hoped would transform American citizens and American governance.

References

Bortis, H. (1999). Political economy, economics, and social sciences. In S. B. Dahiya (Ed.), *The current state of economic science* (pp. 17–42). Rohtak, India: Spellbound Publications.

Bosco, R., Myerson, J., & Ikeda, D. (2009). *Creating Waldens: An east-west conversation on the American renaissance*. Cambridge, MA: Dialogue Path Press.

Bush, P. (1988). Theory of institutional change. In M. Tool (Ed.), *Evolutionary economics* (pp. 125–166). Armonk, NY: M. E. Sharpe.

44 *Theoretical Framework*

Conkin, P. (1968). *Puritans and pragmatists: Eight eminent American thinkers*. USA: Dodd, Mead & Company.

Dewey, J. (1938). *Logic: The theory of inquiry*. New York, NY: Henry Holt and Company.

Dewey, J. (1954). *The public and its problems*. USA: Swallow Press/Ohio University Press Books.

Dewey, J. (1972). *Theory of valuation* (Volume 2, no. 4). Chicago: University of Chicago Press.

Dewey, J. (1993a). Philosophy and Democracy (1919). In D. Morris & I. Shapiro (Eds.), *John Dewey: The political writings* (pp. 38–47). Indianapolis, IN: Hackett Publishing Company.

Dewey, J. (1993b). The ethics of democracy. In D. Morris & I. Shapiro (Eds.), *John Dewey: The political writings* (pp. 59–65). Indianapolis, IN: Hackett Publishing Company.

Dewey, J. (1993c). Creative democracy: The task before us. In D. Morris & I. Shapiro (Eds.), *John Dewey: The political writings* (pp. 240–245). Indianapolis, IN: Hackett Publishing Company.

Dugger, W. (1996). Redefining economics: From market allocation to social provisioning. In C. Whalen (Ed.), *Political economy for the 21st century* (pp. 31–43). Armonk, NY: M. E. Sharp.

Emerson, R. (1983). *Ralph Waldo Emerson: Essays and lectures* (4th ed.). New York: The Library of America.

Forstater, M. (2004). Envisioning provisioning: Adolph Lowe and Heilbroner's worldly philosophy. *Social Research, 71*(2), 399–418.

Foster, J. (1981a). The theory of institutional adjustment. *Journal of Economic Issues, 15*(4), 923–928.

Foster, J. (1981b). Syllabus for problems of modern society: The theory of institutional adjustment. *Journal of Economic Issues, 15*(4), 929–935.

Goldfrank, B. (2012). The World Bank and the globalization of participatory budgeting. *Journal of Public Deliberation, 8*(2), article 7.

Jenco, L. (2003). Thoreau's critique of democracy. *The Review of Politics, 65*(3), 355–381. Retrieved from www.jstor.org/stable/1408930

Lee, F. (2008). Heterodox economics. In S. Durlauf & L. Blume (Eds,), *The new Palgrave Dictionary of economics* (2nd ed.) (Vol. 4) (pp. 2–6). China: Palgrave Macmillan.

Lichtenstein, P. (1983). *An introduction to Post-Keynesian and Marxian theories of value and price* (2nd ed.). New York: M.E. Sharpe.

McIntyre, C. (2008). The politics of Thoreau: A spiritual intent. *The Thoreau Society Bulletin*, (262), 7–9. Retrieved from www.jstor.org/stable/23402794

McWilliams, W. C. (1974). *The idea of fraternity in America* (2nd ed.). USA: University of California Press.

Morris, D., & Shapiro, I. (1993) Editor's introduction. In D. Morris & I. Shapiro (Eds.), *John Dewey: The political writings* (pp. ix–xix). Indianapolis, IN: Hackett Publishing Company.

Power, M. (2004). Social provisioning as a starting point for feminist economics. *Feminist Economics, 10*(3), 133–173.

Ranson, B. (2008, January). Confronting Foster's wildest claim: "Only the instrumental theory of value can be applied!". Presented at *The 2008 annual meeting of the Association for Evolutionary Economics*, New Orleans, LA. Retrieved from http://jfaggfoster.org/RelatedWork.html#BRPaper

Skidmore, M. J. (1998). *Legacy to the world: A study of America's political ideas*. New York: Peter Lang Publishing.

Sturgeon, M. J. (2010). Explorations in institutional economics: The Kansas City approach. Evolutionary Social Theory Work Group 2010 Working Papers. Retrieved from http://cas.umkc.edu/econ/_researchcommunity/evoworkgroup/

Su, C. (2017). From Porto Alegre to New York City: Participatory budgeting and democracy. *New Political Science, 39*(1), 67–75.

Thoreau, H. D. (1996). *Thoreau political writings*, N. L. Rosenblum (Ed.). Cambridge: Cambridge University Press.

Tilman, R. (1987). The neoinstrumental theory of democracy. *Journal of Economic Issues, 21*(3), 1379–1401.

Tool, M. (2000). *Value theory and economic progress: The institutional economics of J. Fagg Foster*. Boston, MA: Kluwer Academic Publishers.

Waller, W. (1982). The evolution of the Veblenian dichotomy: Veblen, Hamilton, Ayres, and Foster. *Journal of Economic Issues, 16*(3), 757–771.

Whitman, W. (1982). *Whitman: Poetry and prose*. New York: The Library of America.

3 How Can the Hypothesis Be Tested?

The hypothesis of this monograph is that as PB processes become more deliberative, more empowered, and greatly expanded, the more participants will experience public happiness, greater understanding of others, greater development of morality, and an increased sense of belonging. As noted in the previous chapter, PBNYC has been chosen to test this hypothesis. In order to test this hypothesis, changes need to be made in both the political and communicative dimensions of a PBNYC process, which should enable these benefits to be realized and also increase participation.

The political dimension has two aspects. The first aspect is that the funding for PBNYC as well as the scope of projects and programs that PBNYC may decide to fund needs to be greatly expanded. PBNYC should be expanded until it becomes a local direct democracy making virtually all local decisions. This is expected to take time because everyone affected will need to be consulted and convinced that this is the best course of action. It is expected that the scope of responsibilities for PBNYC will be slowly expanded.

The other aspect of the political dimension is that city administrations need to be reorganized so that city agencies are under PB in the bureaucratic hierarchy. This will put city agencies in a position to help PB participants develop project proposals and will prevent city agencies from arbitrarily modifying or overruling project proposals. These same city agencies must also be willing and able to implement approved PB projects and provide additional information to PB concerning delays and unexpected costs for these projects. A reorganization of city administration will ensure that this occurs. The reorganization will empower participants by embedding the PB process within local government. This aspect is also expected to take time because city officials will need to be convinced that this will be in their best interests to do so.

Both aspects can be implemented by organizing local civic groups to engage in regular open discussion meetings in order to help mobilize the people to take part in peaceable direct action to address urgent needs of the community. Open discussions with local civic organizations who are working on social issues, which are outside the scope of PB's issues, need to be set up. These organizations could include religious congregations, labor unions, as well as single issue groups. Everyone, in each organization, would have the opportunity of working on other organizations' community priorities and have positive effects on the individuals' and the community's well-being. These organizations can help PB become more fully empowered, help expand the scope of PB's projects, and help increase PB's funding by helping to mobilize peaceful protests.

The communicative dimension means that public communication should be improved in the public forums. Well facilitated public deliberations have many benefits (see Chapter 1) which could be realized by PB processes for both individuals and communities. Facilitators at the level of the working groups, and above, would help ensure that everyone has the opportunity to be heard, no bullying occurs, and in general help keep the discussions on track. I propose that public deliberation be made a goal of PB processes. Additional training would need to be made available for everyone involved in the PB processes.

Democracy is community or associated life. Democracy is a result of cooperation in communities. "In its deepest and richest sense a community must always remain a matter of face-to-face intercourse" (Dewey, 1954, p. 211). Face-to-face public deliberations allows people to change their preferences based on the arguments of others and a re-assessment of their own. Such open and honest face-to-face interaction helps to align an individual's interests with the interests of others.

The first section is a case study of PB in New York City (PBNYC), which is recommended to be the PB process used to test the hypothesis. PBNYC is studied using papers, reports, and documents written by PBNYC. The second section is recommendations for the political dimension of PB, which is based on the previous section as well as the example of PB in Porto Alegre. The third section reports on the conditions needed for public deliberation to occur in PB, which is based primarily on the ethnographic research in *Schools of Democracy*. The next section reviews the recommendations for the communicative dimension of PB, which is based on the previous section as well as the first section. And the last section is about how the recommendations can be implemented and evaluated for PBNYC, which should prove the hypothesis true.

PB in NYC Experience

PB started in New York City in 2011, with four city council members sponsoring it, by allowing PB to allocate about one million dollars each in discretionary capital spending, to each of their districts (Jabola-Carolus, 2017). "By 2014, the number of participating districts grew to twenty-four, making Participatory Budgeting in New York City (PBNYC) the largest PB process in the U.S." (Jabola-Carolus, 2017, p. 110). This section is about the current condition of PBNYC, which needs to be known before recommendations can be made. First, the current amount of facilitator and budget committee training is reviewed. Then, PBNYC's movement toward equity is examined. Next, PBNYC's current criteria for social justice is investigated. And lastly, the administrative oversight of PBNYC is reviewed.

48   *How Can the Hypothesis Be Tested?*

Training Needed

The role of facilitators within budget committees in PBNYC appears to be ad hoc as far as planning for deliberation. "The structure of PB [PBNYC] devolved down to individual budget committees to come up with their own answers" (Gilman, 2012, p. 5). The choice is between focusing on results, which is the number of viable projects, or focusing on the process of quality deliberation. The deciding factor turned out whether the facilitator chose to follow the results model or the process model (Gilman, 2012). It should be noted that the level of facilitator training varied greatly, with some facilitators receiving no training (Gilman, 2012). If public deliberation were a priority, each working group would have a well-trained facilitator whose job is to encourage deliberation.

In a research and evaluation report on PBNYC's cycle 4 (2014–2015), it was reported that "additional emphasis on budget delegate facilitator training and support would be beneficial, as more than half of surveyed facilitators (54%) had not attended a facilitator training and 75% had not joined a facilitator-support conference call" (Community Development Project, 2015, p. 4). This report also pointed out that training of budget delegates varied widely. "Most districts held one orientation meeting for budget delegates. Six districts held two orientations, and two districts reported holding three orientations" (Community Development Project, 2015, p. 4). It is not clear how much training is needed for the delegates. Part of the job of budget delegates at PBNYC is to use the tools given to them that, among other things, help ensure that they consider equity in their deliberations. The evaluation report did say that, "Most surveyed delegate committees utilized tools to consider issues of community need during the project development phase" (Community Development Project, 2015, p. 4). However, the report did not comment on the relationship between the amount of training and the use of these tools.

Equity Goals

In addition to looking at budget delegates and budget delegate facilitators it is important to review how PBNYC is working to be inclusive and fair. "About a third (34%) of assemblies had language support (interpretation or translation) and nearly half (47%) provided food to participants. Fewer districts provided childcare (13%)" (Community Development Project, 2015, p. 4). All these efforts are increasing the number of immigrants who are participating in PBNYC, but more needs to be done. Su wrote, "of all of PBNYC's multiple goals, equity has proven to be the most elusive" (2017, p. 67). This is addressed in the next section.

Public forums need to negate inequalities so that deliberation can occur among equals (Heller & Rao, 2015). PBNYC has procedures to reach out to immigrants and other minorities to try to have better representation within PB meetings. "To level the playing field, we [PBP] have tried to especially recruit leaders who are already mobilizing marginalized communities" (Lerner &

How Can the Hypothesis Be Tested? 49

Secondo, 2012, p. 6). The Participatory Budgeting Project (PBP) is a non-profit that helps initiate and run PB throughout the United States and Canada. PBNYC has hired PBP as a consultant to help administer their PB process. PBP specifically targets underrepresented populations by repeatedly inviting them to participate (Lerner & Secondo, 2012). PBP tries to attract diverse groups of people through the design of the PB processes by holding assemblies near public transportation or better yet within walking distance of everyone (Lerner & Secondo, 2012). "Organizing meetings around events that marginalized groups already attend can also help" (Lerner & Secondo, 2012, p. 6). Attracting diverse groups of people is important because people with diverse opinions are more likely to disagree and engage in deliberation.

New York City has also been working to attract immigrants to vote on PB proposals.

> [D]uring the past four years, participation by immigrants has steadily increased, growing from 19% to more than 28% of all PBNYC voters. Yet, immigrant participation lags compared to their numbers, and there is great variation by immigrants in PB phases and districts.
>
> (Hayduk, Hackett, & Folla, 2017, p. 77)

Thus, PBNYC is moving in the right direction but still has a way to go. Funding for outreach efforts had been at the district level, which varied significantly.

PBNYC has deliberately worked to address traditional barriers to immigrant participation in PB's design.

> First, PBNYC organizers eliminated the citizenship requirement for participation....

> Second, districts are encouraged to use bilingual materials and/or interpreters....

> Third, a few districts and some participating community organizations have provided additional supports ... such as metrocards, childcare, and food, albeit in limited use.

> ...

> Additionally, PB's promise of concrete, if modest, material improvements to their neighborhoods can draw immigrants and immigrant serving community organizations into the process.
>
> (Hayduk et al., 2017, p. 78)

Even though PBNYC is doing a lot, more work is needed. This situation seems to be due to a lack of resources.

50   *How Can the Hypothesis Be Tested?*

Social Justice Method

For PB, social justice refers to the way spending is distributed throughout a metropolitan area. Specifically, depressed areas of a city may need relativity more in terms of infrastructure investment and city services. This was one of the primary components of PB when it was invented in Brazil. First, we will take a quick look at how PB processes in Brazil address social justice. Then, we will examine PBNYC's procedures and tools to address how spending is distributed.

Many cities in Brazil use a "Quality of Life Index" to direct funds to neighborhoods most in need. Each city creates its own formula, which determines what percentage of spending each neighborhood receives. "The Quality of Life Index, based on income, education, physical infrastructure, and social services provided, forms the basis for the distribution of resources" (Wampler, 2007, p. 51). This is meant to ensure that the poorer areas of the city receive more goods and services, from PB.

The social justice aspect of PB was present in PB's initial implementations in Porto Alegre and Belo Horizonte.

> [I]t is possible to document that the poorest regions of Porto Alegre received funding that had not been previously available. It is also possible to confirm that low-income neighborhoods in Belo Horizonte received more resources than did middle- and upper-income neighborhoods.
>
> (Wampler, 2007, p. 51)

Thus, diverting spending to where it is most needed has worked as intended.[1]

While PBNYC does not have a "Quality of Life worked Index" formula, it does have the "Idea Ranking Tool" that budget delegates can use to bring equity into the determination of which proposals to put up for a vote. The PBP developed this tool. "The Idea Ranking Tool is based on three criteria: need, feasibility, and equity. This tool makes public spending more equitable by helping delegates direct resources to where they are most needed" (Participatory Budgeting Project, 2017b, p. 1).

The need, along with the other two criteria, measures each proposal on a scale from one to four. The higher the total score a proposal receives, the more likely the Budget Committee is to recommend funding. Criteria for need includes the following.

> [D]etermine if a project solves an important community problem. The number of times a project was proposed during idea collection ... This project is not already being funded by the city or another source. The project would benefit a large number of people. The project provides a resource that is missing in the community.
>
> (Participatory Budgeting Project, 2017a, p. 2)

The budget delegates can conduct their own research concerning whether a proposal is likely to solve an important community problem (Participatory Budgeting Project, 2017a).

How Can the Hypothesis Be Tested? 51

The feasibility of a proposal is ranked according to whether it meets the following criteria. "Similar projects have been implemented by the city. The project meets eligibility criteria for PB funding. The relevant city agency has stated the project is feasible. There are little or no legal barriers to implement the project" (Participatory Budgeting Project, 2017a, p. 2). Budget proposals might be biased toward what has been done in the past, because city agencies will be more comfortable with what they know.

The equity of a proposal is ranked according to whether the area affected is "low-income, has high enrollment in public assistance, or has other measures of limited resources. The project would direct resources toward many underserved people" (Participatory Budgeting Project, 2017a, p. 3).

The idea-ranking tool can be used in three different stages of a budget committee's work. First, it can be used to create an initial screening of which proposals they will work with. In addition, this tool can identify questions that need to researched and answered before the committee can rank them. Secondly, it can be used to reduce the number of proposals that are sent to city agencies. "Each committee submits 5–10 proposals to Council member staff, who relay proposals to agencies for final review and price estimates" (Participatory Budgeting Project, 2017a, p. 4). The third and final way budget committees can use the idea ranking tool is to help them make the final selection of what will be included on the ballot, after they get feedback from city agencies (Participatory Budgeting Project, 2017b).

The Community Development Project (CDP) at the Urban Justice Center with the PBNYC research team did a research and evaluation report for budget cycle 4 (2014–2015). In this report, "approximately half of reporting facilitators had used district needs maps and district profiles, two-thirds had used a project evaluation matrix, and 80% had made site visits or done field research" (Community Development Project, 2015). An earlier version of the idea-ranking tool was called the project evaluation matrix. This shows that a majority of budget committees were doing field research and using the project evaluation matrix in their research and decisions.

Interface with City Agencies

In the previous chapter it was found that the city agencies who have been charged with approving and implementing PBNYC decisions are changing, or in some cases ignoring, the PBNYC decisions. Also, there is a computer interface where people may bypass the public forums and directly submit requests to the city agencies. First, the computer interface was found to be discriminatory. And secondly, the face-to-face meetings are where the intangible benefits of PB are realized. Thus, the computer interface should be abandoned.

The administrative control of PBNYC shifted after the 2014 election of city officials. "A total of twenty-one Council Members who pledged to sponsor PB were elected or re-elected, a 133% increase" (Jabola-Carolus, 2017, p. 115), out of 51 Council Members. In addition, Mark-Viverito, one of the original sponsors

52 How Can the Hypothesis Be Tested?

of PBNYC, won the City Council Speaker seat (Jabola-Carolus, 2017). "Mark-Viverito committed to devote central City Council resources for PB implementation" (Jabola-Carolus, 2017, p. 115). These reforms included changes to the Steering Committee.

The Steering Committee "determines basic rules of the process, influences resource allocation for PB implementation, and oversees PBNYC's adherence to overarching goals and principles" (Jabola-Carolus, 2017, p. 113). "The Steering Committee included representatives from the Council Members' offices, district-level community-based organizations, and citywide non-governmental groups" (Jabola-Carolus, 2017, p. 115). After the 2014 reforms, the duties of the Steering Committee were changed. In the 2014–2015 cycle, the reforms "moved the locus of citywide PB coordination from civil society to government" (Jabola-Carolus, 2017, p. 116).

The reforms had mixed results. Of course, devoting City Council resources to PB was very helpful. "By carving out space for PB staff in central city offices, the Council Speaker provided greater administrative stability and infused PB with normalcy and growth potential that shoestring CSOs could never provide" (Jabola-Carolus, 2017, p. 117).

> Alongside these gains, however, challenges emerged that threatened PBNYC's impacts. Some members expressed concern about diminished capacity for evaluation.... Others noted that resources for targeted outreach also failed to adequately rise, resulting in a net decrease in per-district outreach funding. One of the clearest losses, however, was a loosening of popular control in the Steering Committee.
>
> (Jabola-Carolus, 2017, p. 117)

The role of the Steering Committee had substantially changed.

> This approach [the effect of the reforms] reinforced the two main functions left to the Steering Committee in the new division of labor: monitoring the citywide coordination efforts, and in effect, serving as a focus group as the central staff built technologies to streamline PB implementation.
>
> (Jabola-Carolus, 2017, p. 121)

The Steering committee pushed to have the process reorganized. During cycle five (2015–2016), "With Speaker Mark-Viverito's approval, the positions of committee co-chairs was restored, to enable greater civil society control of agendas and deliberations" (Jabola-Carolus, 2017, p. 122). This resulted in greater participation by the non-profits.

The strong support from the new City Council Speaker helps the growth potential for PBNYC. While city agencies may be adapting to PB slower than was hoped, they are making changes to support PB. A letter writing campaign was started advocating that the mayor play a bigger role in PBNYC. Improving the quality and scope of PBNYC is always ongoing.

How Can the Hypothesis Be Tested? 53

I have no doubt that by the time this book is published some positive changes will have been made that improve communications between the PBNYC process and the city agencies that they work with. The future control of PB needs to be closely monitored. Politicians can be allies. They may also have their own agendas. However, unless the city's administrative bureaucratic hierarchy is restructured such that PBNYC is above the agencies it works with, the danger of PBNYC's decisions being arbitrarily modified will always be present. The following section addresses this issue.

Recommendations for Political Dimension

The political dimension of PB empowers participants to govern themselves. The recommendations in this section should help participants realize their potential political and economic power. Obviously, the city agencies play a significant role in the PB process. And the previous chapter demonstrates that an institutional adjustment needs to occur such that the city agencies will no longer be able to arbitrarily change or ignore PBNYC decisions.

As noted in Chapter 1, it was easier to expand PB around the world without insisting on municipal reorganization. However, we see that without it, participants in PBNYC are not truly empowered. This is what Baiocchi and Ganuza referred to as the sovereignty dimension of PB (2017). In this monograph, the political dimension is defined as the sovereignty dimension (city administrative reorganization) plus an expansion of PBNYC until it becomes a local direct democracy in order for all of the potential benefits to be realized. Both aspects of the political dimension can be achieved with open-ended discussions with representatives of other civic organizations about social issues, which are outside the scope of PBNYC. These open-ended discussions should lead to peaceable direct actions, which benefit the community, individual participants, and PBNYC.

History has shown that "success [of PB] is more likely when there is limited resistance on the part of opposition parties, the local legislature, and state bureaucrats" (Jabola-Carolus, 2017, p. 111). It always seems to be a case of political will, which public opinion intensity seems to determine. "Most visible in this case [PBNYC] is bureaucratic resistance to change and to non-expert participation, which presents a problem not only for PB administration but also for popular control" (Jabola-Carolus, 2017, p. 123). At least part of the reason that city officials in NYC may be reluctant to allow PBNYC participants to make decisions instead of municipal bureaucracies is a belief in expert rule. As noted in Chapter 1, this is a part of managerialism. The trouble is that what experts want may not coincide with what the people want. Experts need to be consulted. But that does not mean that the experts need to have the final say. Resistance from city bureaucracies can be overcome with a reorganization of the city's administrative organizations. The first subsection looks at how Porto Alegre reorganized their city's bureaucracy in order to empower PB participants, which could be used as a template for New York City.

54 *How Can the Hypothesis Be Tested?*

Resistance from political parties and politicians can be overcome with a shift in public opinion. The second subsection is about starting open-ended discussions with local civic organizations to discuss and act on their priorities. This should result in PBNYC gaining allies in a campaign to empower PBNYC by reorganizing the city bureaucracy as well as expanding PBNYC until it becomes a local direct democracy. And it should also result in a shift in public opinion in support of an empowered and expanded PBNYC.

Bureaucratic Reorganization

We have seen that the current state of affairs in PBNYC includes city agencies routinely overruling parts, or the entirety, of PBNYC projects, which the PB assemblies and budget committees have approved. In many cases this is due to the elevation of the agencies' priorities over those of the PB participants.

The budget delegates in PBNYC do not have any power over the city agencies. PBNYC is not part of the city's administrative structure and thus has no power within it.

> Notably, in contrast to Porto Alegre and other notable cases of PB, no municipal offices were created or restricted to manage PB [PBNYC] inputs or mobilize participation. Instead, the administrative model during the first three years leaned on low-capacity, decentralized city staff, and under-resourced CSOs.
>
> (Jabola-Carolus, 2017, p. 115)

A reorganization of municipal administration is needed to more fully empower PBNYC participants.

The reorganization of NYC's administrative structure appears to be necessary in order to empower participants and realize PBNYC's full potential. "[T]he absence of strong civil society pressure may contribute to the lack of political will to pursue broader reforms and alleviate bureaucratic constraints" (Jabola-Carolus, 2017, p. 124). The next subsection is about a recommendation that addresses this issue. Many civic organizations working together could get a surprising amount of change implemented. They could be the driving force behind a reorganization of the city's administration that provides a prominent place for PBNYC in New York City's bureaucratic hierarchy.

Open-ended Discussions

Working with other social organizations can increase the individuals' and communities' well-being by working on the priorities of various social organizations. Of course, one of PBNYC's priorities should be that they become more fully integrated into the municipal administration. In part, this means that city agencies are under PB in the bureaucratic hierarchy. This will truly empower the PB participants. Another one of PBNYC's priorities should be to increase its

How Can the Hypothesis Be Tested? 55

funding and increase the scope of projects it is able to vote upon. This will further empower participants who will be able to direct more of the city's spending. As more people demand these reforms, the more city officials will realize that it is in their best interest to vote for such a popular program.

I propose that representatives from PBNYC have regularly scheduled meetings with representatives of civic-minded organizations and engage in deliberations about local social issues. These open-ended discussions would be about social issues that are outside the scope of the PB process. Of course, trained facilitators would need to be present to help deliberations proceed smoothly. These representatives could then discuss the same issues within their organizations. The purpose would be to motivate more people to engage in public deliberations and to get more people involved in their communities. Participants in open-ended discussion meetings could discuss anything, including, but not limited to, school dropout rates, reforming local government to be more responsive to the people, police issues, homelessness, local minimum wages, local jobs[2], or integration of former convicts into the community. Invited social organizations would include those who are working on some of these issues. In addition, inviting church groups and labor unions along with other concerned civic groups should make this group more representative.

These proposed open-ended discussions would seem to violate one of Talpin's four conditions for deliberation, namely stakes (discussed in the next section). Since these discussions would be outside the scope of PBNYC, no funding would be available. Since the participants would not be making binding spending decisions, why would they consider the deliberations important?

Working to achieve consensus could be the goal that motivates people to participate in a public deliberation.

> Unanimity is also most likely to yield a better informed and considered group opinion because the need for participants to find common ground gives them strong incentives to share information and opinions, gain knowledge, and give each view a fair hearing (Bächtiger, Grönlund, & Setälä, 2014; Karpowitz & Mendelberg, 2014).
>
> (Abdullah, Karpowitz, & Raphael, 2016, p. 26)

Once they agree that consensus is important, they might be willing to put in more effort than usual during deliberations.

What will happen when they do reach consensus? Without a source of funding, what would be the point? "[U]nanimity may be more likely than majority rule to mobilize participants to further action on behalf of the group's conclusions because consensus strengthens each member's commitment to the collective verdict" (Karpowitz & Raphael, 2014)" (Abdullah et al., 2016. p. 26). The participants would work together with their social organizations to raise awareness and work for the needed change they all agreed to.

It is not unheard of for PB to have open-ended discussions. Baiocchi studied the effect existing social capital had on open-ended discussions in two Porto

56 *How Can the Hypothesis Be Tested?*

Alegre districts. In the district with less existing social capital, these open-ended discussions would sometimes deteriorate into personal arguments (Baiocchi, 2003). Quickly defusing personal hostility helps to maintain and encourage a sense of belonging to a community. If these open-ended discussions work as intended, it would connect PB with other social organizations advocating for community issues, which has been called for by some (Baiocchi & Ganuza, 2017; Lerner & Pape, 2016). Perhaps some of the social organization's priorities could be incorporated into an expanded PB process.

Open-ended discussions, by generating a sense of belonging to a community and by building social capital, would help build the capacity of individuals and the communities. The first step in helping marginalized communities is for members of the community to develop a capacity to aspire. Appadurai wrote,

> [T]he experiential limitations in subaltern populations, on the capacity to aspire, tend to create a binary relationship to core cultural values, negative and skeptical at one pole, overattached at the other....Of course, the objective is to increase the capacity for the third posture, the posture of "voice," the capacity to debate, contest, inquire, and participate critically.
>
> (2004, pp. 69–70)

Of course, the open-ended discussions and the PB process could not only build the capacity to aspire, it could build the capacity of people to accomplish concrete things for their communities.

If several civic organizations come together and act together in open-ended discussions, their influence would grow. They would then be creating social capital on a larger scale. The different social organizations could help each other reach their goals. In the case of PB, the other organizations could campaign to include PBNYC as part of the city's administrative structure, expand the scope of PB projects, and increase the amount of money that is available for PBNYC.

This is important because the scope of PB processes are limited, in both the types of projects and the amount of money that is available. "Without careful expansion, PBNYC can act as a release valve for frustrated residents and help some to address small scale needs, but it will not necessarily help to address redistribution or equity" (Su, 2017, p. 74). Open-ended discussions could help PBNYC make connections with other social organizations who will want to help campaign to empower and expand PBNYC.

Conditions Needed for Public Deliberation

Deliberation does not usually emerge spontaneously (Talpin, 2011). In order for people to be able to deliberate, they need to deliberate as equals (Heller & Rao, 2015). It is necessary to neutralize the effects of inequalities within the public forum to enhance the deliberative process. This is addressed in the procedures subsection. As the result of ethnographic research of three PB processes in Europe, Talpin found that there are four conditions for deliberation to occur,

How Can the Hypothesis Be Tested? 57

which are procedures, disagreement, leaders, and stakes (2011, p. 140). In addition to these four conditions, I have added a fifth subsection about equity.

There may seem to be a conflict between equality and equity. However, both can and should co-exist in a deliberative democratic forum.

> At high level of abstraction, we can conceive of the "democratic" part of deliberative democracy as comprised of *equality* in opportunities for participation, and *equity* in processes and outcomes. Within the context of democratic theory, *equality* almost always refers constitutionally to rights and empowerments that attach to citizenship.
>
> (Moscrop & Warren, 2016, p. 2)

Most people in the United States see the value of equality in opportunities. However, some might believe that equality is sufficient for people to pull themselves up by their bootstraps, so to speak. "Yet, formal equalities are quite compatible with substantive inequities that can undermine the democratic dimensions of deliberative processes" (Moscrop & Warren, 2016, p. 4). For example, everyone may have equal opportunity to attend a public forum, but some might not be able to afford the bus fare. Furthermore, some people might need to have an interpreter. "Ideally, equality enables equity: equal distribution of empowerments such as votes, rights, and opportunities for voice should enable citizens to press for equity" (Moscrop & Warren, 2016, p. 2). Thus, incorporating both equality and equity into the design produces the best outcome for deliberative democracy.

Procedures

"One of the crucial prerequisites for the emergence of deliberation is the organization of the discussion" (Talpin, 2011, p. 141). In order to encourage organized group discussion, the speakers and the audience should be at the same level, for the symbolic representation of equal power. Of course, everyone should be able to easily see and hear each other. Thus, PB assemblies are usually arranged in circles. Also, the size of the discussion groups is important. If the group size is too large it can impede the quality of the discussion; working groups should be formed based on thematic areas, with four to ten people (Talpin, 2011).

Increasing the number of viewpoints heard can also encourage the emergence of deliberation. The facilitator could organize "turn-taking" with a set number of minutes for each speaker. People running over their time would need to sanctioned (Talpin, 2011). One possible way to get a person to yield their time if they are running significantly long, would be to pre-arrange with some people in the assembly to help talk down someone who is refusing to yield the floor. Some people may never before have had a chance to speak out, and they may have many pent-up grievances. The idea of getting a large number of people to speak up is that disagreement will surface, which is a precondition for the emergence of deliberation.

58 *How Can the Hypothesis Be Tested?*

However, there are potential drawbacks to using the discursive procedure of "turn-taking."

> This discursive procedure is not institutionalized however, and therefore depends on the style of the facilitators. Furthermore, some problems remain with this discursive trick. It becomes indeed increasingly difficult for people to express dissent as a certain number of persons have already expressed their views.
>
> (Talpin, 2011, p. 143)

People are reluctant to express a viewpoint openly that is different from the majority opinion.

The Rome Municipio XI PB process uses a simple report to organize discussion and increase the chances for deliberation to emerge for issues that were not on the agenda. After items on the agenda had been covered, there was often time for other issues to be discussed.

> Participants come up with issues that were not initially on the agenda, generally related to personal troubles they have, that actually motivated their presence at the meeting. What follows is a messy discussion, where lay citizens, upset at having remained silent for so long, express themselves aggressively, while elected representatives and civil servants try to answer the questions and evoke possible solutions.
>
> (Talpin, 2011, p. 143)

Hostile confrontations were often the result. The solution for this situation was to introduce a simple report that must be completed.

> People have first to state and define the problem they identified. Then, in a second column, that have to propose a solution to the problem. Discussion generally occurs at both stages, to define the problem correctly, and then to evaluate possible courses of action to solve it. A report is thus written at the end of each meeting for each thematic area, and then addressed to the technical services of the Municipio, who are required to provide an answer.
>
> (Talpin, 2011, pp. 143–144)

This simple report forced people to slow down and do what was needed, in the order it needed to be done. The report opened up the possibility of deliberation taking place. The technical services looked at such things as whether something was already planned to address the issue, whether it was technically feasible, and how much the suggested solution might cost. At the next meeting, the technical services report would be used as the basis for further discussion (Talpin, 2011). "The organization of the discussion appears, therefore, as a crucial element for the emergence of deliberation" (Talpin, 2011, p. 144). Considerable thought has to go into the planning of a meeting in order to create an atmosphere that is

How Can the Hypothesis Be Tested? 59

favorable for deliberation. This simple report also is a reminder that thinking about ways to enhance the deliberative process is ongoing, and thus is never finished.

Disagreement

Disagreement is the second condition for deliberation. People must be willing and able to disagree in public meetings before deliberation can occur. "Heterogeneity and the diversity of views are necessary, but not sufficient conditions for the emergence of deliberation. What matters however is the discursive expression of diversity" (Talpin, 2011, p. 144). A group of people with diverse viewpoints is needed, and they must be willing to express these viewpoints.

A facilitator's style can help people express themselves. After they have formed into working groups, a facilitator can have participants introduce themselves and give a little personal information before asking for their priorities. "Most of the time people consider opinions to be private matters" (Talpin, 2011, p. 146). Talpin argued, "[I]t appears inappropriate to contradict anonymous strangers (Eliasoph, 1998; Conover, Crew, & Searing, 2002; Duchesne & Haegel, 2006)" (Talpin, 2011, p. 146). Thus, people may be more willing to express their opinions to, and disagree with, a friend, or at least an acquaintance.

"The public expression of disagreement is a difficult move" (Talpin, 2011, p. 146). Some of the procedures, such as small group size, sitting in a circle, and turn taking, can help people speak up when they disagree. In addition, community leaders can be important for the expression of divergent views.

Leaders

The presence of leaders is the third condition for deliberation. "Activists and political party militants have a decisive influence on the quality of PB discussions. Holding strong preferences, they have the cultural and political resources necessary for the expression of dissent" (Talpin, 2011, p. 146). Activists have the knowledge and self-confidence to publicly express and defend their views. Talpin wrote, "it seems that in Rome and Seville deliberation could not have happened without the commitment of local militants" (2011, p. 147). Of course, it would seem to be important to have activists representing different positions.

Morsang-sur-Orge was the third PB process studied by Talpin. "In Morsang-sur-Orge, given the presence of elected representatives in public meetings, dissent and conflict generally emerged between citizens and members of the municipal majority" (Talpin, 2011, p. 147). However, "the presence of politicians in the discussion transforms it into a bargaining process" (Talpin, 2011, p. 148). Instead of deliberation taking place between equal citizens, you have bargaining with the authorities (Talpin, 2011). Thus, it seems that community activists are needed for deliberation to happen; and care needs to be taken whenever politicians are present to ensure their presence does not interfere with deliberation.

60 How Can the Hypothesis Be Tested?

Stakes

The fourth condition for deliberation involves stakes. The fact that the end result of PB discussions and deliberations are to make binding spending decisions changes the importance of the deliberations. "Stakes push people to express their views – not keep them private – if they want ... to make a difference in on the final decision" (Talpin, 2011, p. 149). Of course, the amount of money available makes a difference in how motivated people are to participate. But also important are the types of projects that PB is allowed to fund.

In the United States, some PB processes are more limited than others regarding how the money can be spent. PBNYC is able to fund more popular projects than Chicago PB, which may, in part, explain why PBNYC has more participants. "Unlike in Chicago, however, the NYC capital funds are often used for public housing and schools, which has fueled more grassroots interest" (Lerner & Secondo, 2012, p. 4). Money needs to be available to fund projects that are of interest to the community in order to motivate people to get involved.

Equity

If public deliberation becomes a priority for PB, it is logical to place a greater emphasis on equity. A focus on equity will help to level the playing field for traditionally marginalized groups, which would include encouragement for marginalized groups to attend PB meetings. Since traditionally marginalized people will likely have different opinions than groups that have access to power, this should add to the diversity of opinions at PB meetings, which is a necessary but not sufficient condition for deliberation to occur.

Another benefit of including traditionally disenfranchised groups is helping to ensure that social justice is addressed by redistributing spending to those most in need. This was a contributing factor to PB's rapid expansion throughout Latin America. Even though many PB processes around the world no longer have a strong social justice aspect, there are good reasons to include equity and social justice in PB.

Importantly, the application of Wampler's four principles of PB (voice, vote, social justice, and oversight) may lead to a virtuous cycle with everyone involved increasingly benefiting. Wampler wrote:

> My research over a number of years indicates that PB's impact on democratic legitimacy is directly correlated with the degree to which each specific PB program adheres to the four principles. If the government and citizens commit to all four principles, a virtuous cycle is initialed in which the benefits of voice, vote, social justice, and oversight are mutually reinforcing.
>
> (2012, p. 9)

Thus, a focus on equity leading to social justice, given the implementation of the other three principles, could result in benefits not only for marginalized citizens, but for the local government and the PB process as well. Of course, everyone participating in the deliberative process would receive the individual benefits, as described elsewhere.

Recommendations for Communicative Dimension

Improving public communication within PB assemblies and meetings is an ongoing necessity. People need to be able to clearly state and defend their opinions concerning public spending in order to influence the outcome of a vote. And yet, in 2016, when Leighninger and Rinehart reported about the state of deliberation in North American PB processes. They found that none had public deliberation as one of their process goals. Some of the process goals they found were inclusiveness, being an educational process, and increased collaboration (pp. 8–9). Public deliberation would also be an excellent goal.

Public deliberation, when done correctly, can change individual preferences, which can converge during the course of deliberation. From Chapter 1, we learned that public deliberation can help clarify, inform, foster cooperation, and promote empathy. I recommend that public deliberation become a goal for PBNYC. As people start to experience the benefits of public deliberation, it is likely that participation will increase as others learn about it by word-of-mouth.

The first subsection makes communication recommendations specific to the PBNYC experience, as reported in the first section of this chapter. The second subsection makes communication recommendations based on research by Talpin as well as research on communication within working groups.

Specific to PBNYC Experience

If public deliberation is going to become a goal of PBNYC, more will be expected from the facilitators. Currently, facilitators are volunteers (New York City Council, 2018). I propose that they become employees since they will be expected to do more.

For example, I recommend that facilitator training, as well as all other training, be face-to-face, as opposed to conference calls. This will require a greater commitment from the facilitators. In the first section, we learned from the 2015 Community Development Project report that only about 25% of facilitators had joined a facilitator-support conference call (Community Development Project, 2015). It is easier to require employees attend meetings than volunteers. In addition, Schutz's research, which is discussed in a later chapter, shows that we can genuinely understand another person's point of view in face-to-face interactions (Walsh, 1967). Part of this understanding comes from being in the physical presence of another person. There is much more information communicated in face-to-face interactions than over the phone. Thus, I recommend that all facilitator meetings be face-to-face.

One of the fundamental keys to the success of PB is that the face-to-face interactions tend to build social capital, which enables the PB processes and PB

62 How Can the Hypothesis Be Tested?

participants to build on successes and allows participants to increasingly realize the benefits of public deliberation. Thus, I recommend that online submission of PBNYC proposals be discontinued. Another reason for discontinuing this process is that it seems to have had a discriminatory effect, as noted in the PBNYC experience section. All project proposals should go through the same process, which includes face-to-face discussions, before they are submitted to city agencies. This would seem to be a logical result of making public deliberation a goal of PBNYC.

Another benefit of making public deliberation a goal is that it could indirectly provide the needed resources to meet the equity goal. Once PBNYC makes public deliberation a goal and they start moving toward it, people will learn how to better express their views in public, they will become more effective at it, and they will increasingly realize the benefits of public deliberation. As these results spread by word-of-mouth, PB will likely become more popular. And as more people participate in PBNYC, the local politicians will feel increasing pressure to fully fund PB, which seems to be the only reason PBNYC has not met its equity goals. However, until the city pays for the incentives needed to attract traditionally disenfranchised groups, funding will need to temporary come from other sources, which is covered in the next section, Implementation and Measurement.

Also, more funding is needed not only to pay facilitators, but to pay for additional training as well. The first section in this chapter documents the need for additional and consistent training. The following subsection recommends additional duties for facilitators.

Talpin and Working Group Research

This subsection starts with recommendations for the communicative dimension of PB, which are suggested by Talpin's research. Then research is presented concerning the composition and management of smaller working group discussions. It is recommended that the increased training for facilitators include these insights. As was stated earlier, public deliberation is something that needs to be constantly monitored and most probably will always be a work in-process.

Many people may need training in public speaking. Talpin's study found this to be a barrier.

> People have, first of all, to acquire the self-confidence to speak up and express themselves, clearly in front of the assembly. This constitutes a first hurdle, as lower participation in the discussion meetings (working groups in Rome, delegate meetings in Seville) indicates.
>
> (2011, p. 164)

If public deliberation is made a goal of PB, training in public speaking should be made available.

In addition to public speaking, it would be helpful to instruct people on the style of grammar expected in a PB assembly. Talpin found that there is certain grammar that is acceptable, and some that is not acceptable at PB assemblies. For example, "it seems that there is a certain consensus around the world – mostly in Europe, Latin, and North America – on the value of detachment and practically (consensus coming from similar historical and structural evolutions) in the public realm" (Talpin, 2011, p. 159). Talpin found that "PB discursive interactions are ruled by three main norms: Common-good orientation – Non-political discourses – [and] Practicality" (Talpin, 2011, p. 164). Talpin gives an example of a man, Christian, at a Morsang-sur-Orge PB meeting. They were discussing the organization of traffic near a school. Everyone was emphasizing the children's safety. Christian seemed to brush aside concerns for the children and spoke about the need for parking. "[H]e was sanctioned for not having respected the ruling public grammar, which makes 'kids' security' the highest value" (2011, p. 165). Christian's proposal was dismissed without any real consideration. "At the following meeting however, a few weeks later, Christian presented his arguments in a different way, and obtained much better results (2011, pp. 165–166). Christian had re-framed his proposal to include concern for the children.

The reason these norms are important is that if someone does not adopt to them, they will likely become discouraged and leave, because the grammar is enforced by shaming. "The will to avoid shame, or more slightly, public embarrassment, appeared as a strong explanation of self-change in the studied cases" (Talpin, 2011, p. 165). However, there are problems with this practice. First, it is unfair to shame a well-intentioned person. Secondly, many people may not change; they may just leave.

> The only data available are for the Roman case, where turnover rates are extremely high. In 2004, 68.5 per cent of the participants declared they had not participated in the PB the year before. About half of 2003 participants stopped after one year.
>
> (Talpin, 2011, p. 168)

It would be easy to instruct all newcomers on the importance of framing an issue. This should be part of the training.

Before each neighborhood assembly, people could be invited to public speaking and deliberation workshops. People will need to be provided training in the art of deliberation. Pateman wrote, "the central claim of deliberative democratic theorists: that individuals should always be prepared to defend their moral and political arguments and claims with reasons, and be prepared to deliberate with others about the reasons they provide" (2012, p. 8). Due to inequality in education and experience, many people may not feel prepared to publicly deliberate. Thus, providing training for anyone who would like it is necessary.

In addition to training the participants in the PB assemblies, there needs to a consistently high level of training for facilitators. Facilitators need to make sure there is no coercion; everyone has a chance to speak, as well as ensuring that discussions do not become personal.

The results of Talpin's research concerning the conditions needed for deliberation, as reported in the previous section, should be included in the training for

64 *How Can the Hypothesis Be Tested?*

facilitators. This includes inviting activists to help stimulate deliberation until the training of participants to deliberate produces tangible results.

Part of the facilitator's training should be ongoing so they can compare notes on what seems to be working. One example would be the situation discussed in the Conditions for Deliberation section, about encouraging disagreement. Recall, from the previous section, that some people are reluctant to share their views with or disagree with strangers. Facilitators could experiment with giving people different amounts of time to talk about themselves to see what, if any, differences they see in the number of people who are willing to deliberate. If facilitators worked together, they could reduce their learning curve concerning how much time it takes people not to feel like strangers and open up with others.

Another area of facilitator training would be the importance of how people are divided into working groups. For best deliberative results, care should be taken when dividing people into smaller working groups. Research finds that highly educated white males speak more often and have greater influence over decisions (Abdullah et al., 2016).

> Democratic theorists have long recognized that members of less privileged groups need to confer among themselves in civil society associations in order to contribute autonomously and effectively to discussion in the wider public sphere (Fraser, 1992; Mansbridge 1996; Sunstein, 2000).
>
> (Abdullah et al., 2016, pp. 1–2)

Thus, marginalized groups should deliberate in their own affinity groups, to advance equity (Abdullah et al., 2016). Affinity or enclave groups refers to people with similar influences and perspectives.

In public deliberation, it is important that everyone have an equal opportunity to speak.

> [P]eople with less education or income, of lower social status, immigrants conversing in their second tongue, and women can be less likely to speak or influence others in mixed groups (Black, 2015; Gerber, 2015; Han, Schenck-Hamlin, & Schenck-Hamlin, 2015; Hansen, 2010; Himmelroos, 2014).
>
> (Abdullah et al., 2016, p. 6)

That is why these groups should develop their ideas among themselves before participating in the larger public forum. This strategy can help ensure that a diversity of viewpoints is expressed, which is needed for deliberation to occur.

> Not only are they likely to assemble their own experiential knowledge more effectively than in mixed settings, but they are likely to formulate different questions for experts and officials, which can elicit information about the effects of policy options on less privileged sectors of society.
>
> (Abdullah et al., 2016, pp. 16–17)

How Can the Hypothesis Be Tested? 65

This might be the only way for all members of the community to be able to express themselves as equals within a public forum.

Since the people in these enclaves share similar influences and perspectives, it might appear that they would all share the same viewpoints. However, facilitators can draw out any differences.

> [F]acilitators can foster exploration of similarities and differences of experience and understandings within the group. Moderators can question those who may try to impose a single identity or set of interests on the enclave, and encourage each participant to articulate their own understanding of their social locations.
>
> (Abdullah et al., 2016, p. 26)

The role of the facilitator is critical in the composition of working groups, as well as encouraging everyone to speak their own mind within each group.

Implementation and Measurement

The hypothesis of this monograph is that as PB processes become more deliberative, more empowered, and greatly expanded the more participants will experience public happiness, greater understanding of others, greater development of morality, and an increased sense of belonging. In order to fully test this hypothesis, all the recommended changes need to be implemented. This section starts with the expected source of funding needed to implement the recommendations for both the communicative and the political dimensions of PBNYC. Then, how the results will be measured is examined. For the communicative dimension it is recommended that at first only the deliberations in working groups be evaluated because that is where most of the deliberations will occur. Then, after that is evaluated look at doing a separate evaluation for the larger public assemblies, if needed. The quality of public deliberation can be measured using the Debilitative Transformative Moments (DTM) index. To measure the effect of the reforms in both the communicative and political dimensions, a short questionnaire can be given to PBNYC participants using unipolar fully labeled five-point scales. This questionnaire measures the four intangible benefits in the hypothesis. The recommended participant questionnaire is in the appendix.

Implementation

For the communicative dimension, the hypothesis can be tested by obtaining the funding to fully implement, and measure the effect of, all recommended changes that will improve the quality of public deliberation for PBNYC. First, nonprofits promoting democracy need to be approached to gauge their level of interest in providing grants. The nonprofits providing the funds would need to hire someone to work with PBNYC. Of course, the cooperation, coordination, and help from PBNYC and the nonprofits who help administer it is extremely important. Since

66   *How Can the Hypothesis Be Tested?*

PBNYC will not have to pay for the recommended changes, it is likely that the New York City (NYC) council and the nonprofits who help administer PBNYC will help support this democratic experiment. Given PB's potential benefits described in this monograph, it should be achievable to obtain the needed funds. PBNYC may provide a unique opportunity to create an environment where public deliberations can thrive due to the diverse population, the active civic groups, and the enthusiasm people have for PBNYC. "The conditions under which deliberative democracy thrives may be quite rare and difficult to achieve" (Thompson, 2008, p. 500). This experiment could prove that all the benefits of deliberative democracy are real.

> There would be no guarantee that deliberative democracy would be vindicated, but with a more discriminating and wide-ranging analysis of the conditions that promote or impede it, we would have a clearer sense of its place in democratic theory and practice.
>
> (Thompson, 2008, p. 500)

Encouraging public deliberation could provide part of the answer to the question of how can we revitalize democracy? The other part of the answer could be found in the actions needed to empower the political dimension of PBNYC.

For the political dimension, it is anticipated that a small group of people is needed to contact, help coordinate, and bring together representatives of all, or most of, the civic organizations of NYC to participate in open-ended discussions. The same person hired to coordinate with PBNYC to improve public deliberation could hire a staff to improve the political aspect of PBNYC. Obviously, regularly scheduled meeting places need to be secured for the representatives of the civic groups to implement the open-ended discussions. If funding is available, it would be worthwhile to measure the quality of deliberations the same way as for PBNYC. Representatives of civic organizations would be expected to be more knowledgeable about the issues. Also, as mentioned before, the open-ended discussions would be striving for consensus while PBNYC may not be. Thus, it would be interesting to compare the quality of deliberations.

The topics of discussion, in the open-ended discussions, would be outside the scope of PBNYC and most will be chosen by the civic groups. The purpose of these meetings is to increase social capital using public deliberation and the use of non-violent direct action in order to accomplish community goals. The community goals would most likely be the priorities of the attending civic organizations. Two planned topics would be priorities and directly affect PBNYC. The first one is that in order to more fully empower PBNYC participants, a campaign needs to be discussed, planned, and implemented to persuade the NYC administration to reorganize its bureaucratic hierarchy. The purpose of such a reorganization is to place PBNYC in the hierarchy above the city agencies that PBNYC works with. This will prevent city agencies from placing their priorities over those of PBNYC. This was the model in Porto Alegre, Brazil. The other planned topic for these open-ended discussions that effects PBNYC will be discussing,

How Can the Hypothesis Be Tested? 67

planning, and implementing an ongoing effort to expand the funding and the scope of projects that PBNYC may consider.

After each open-ended discussion its participants could, contingent on funding, report to neighborhood assemblies to discuss ideas from the open-ended discussion group and generate new ideas. Of course, these neighborhood assemblies would be the source of power needed to get things done. Otherwise, the people representing the civic groups would report back to their respective organizations for feedback and support.

It is hoped that PBNYC will send representatives to these open-ended discussions. However, if the NYC council initially objects to an administrative reorganization, it may not be possible for PBNYC to be involved in a campaign to change the bureaucratic hierarchy. But perhaps they could still be involved in talks about expanding the funding and scope of responsibilities for PBNYC. Official PBNYC representation would not be needed initially. However, the non-profits that help administer PBNYC would hopefully all be represented. It would be in the civic groups' best interests to push for a local direct democracy where their priorities would have better chances of becoming priorities of the city. Also, once PBNYC sees that the open-ended discussions can produce public direct actions that have the effect of expanding its funding and scope of activities, it is likely that PBNYC will want to be a part of discussions with the open-ended discussions members about the future of PBNYC. In the face of over-whelming public support, local politicians will likely want to become associated with the campaign to improve and expand PBNYC.

Increasing the funding for PBNYC and expanding the scope of its projects may enable civic groups to get action on some of their priorities through PBNYC. Residents of the city would be increasingly motivated to participate in PBNYC the larger the budget they had to work with and the greater latitude they had to fund projects and programs to help their community. Since PBNYC has proven to be popular, many local politicians should support the expansion of PBNYC.

Obviously, it may take time to convince local politicians to strengthen PBNYC by reorganizing the city's bureaucratic hierarchy, increase funding, and expand the scope of their responsibilities. This is not a quick fix. But, considering the potential benefits, it would be well worth the effort.

Measurement

There is not a standard recipe that can be used to increase deliberation in all situations. "One cannot simply say at a general level that such and such institutional, psychological, and cultural measures should be taken to increase deliberation. One rather needs to look at the specific situation" (Steiner, 2012, p. 217). This is one reason why deliberation is rare. Steiner wrote, "It is hard and detailed work to investigate in specific cases what can be done to increase the chances of good deliberation" (2012, p. 217). How then would one proceed to increase the quantity and the quality of deliberation in specific instances?

68 *How Can the Hypothesis Be Tested?*

First, the researcher must become familiar with the social environment of the participants in the case being studied. "If one wishes to give recommendations, one has to immerse oneself in the historical, cultural, social, economic, and political context to give meaningful advice" (Steiner, 2012, p. 217). And more importantly, the advice of the participants should be sought. "I [Steiner] hope that positive feedback will result in the sense that deliberation about increased deliberation will lead to a higher level of deliberation, which in turn will help deliberation about further increases in deliberation, and so on" (Steiner, 2012, pp. 217–218). Thus, it is anticipated that this results in a virtuous cycle improving deliberation with, and among, the participants. Something else to keep in mind is that many times people telling a story to illustrate his or her point will help the deliberative discourse.

It may not seem that story-telling should have a place in public deliberations. However, as Steiner wrote, "The moderator should also allow stories to be told. Even if stories are off-topic, they may help to loosen up the atmosphere in the discussion group" (2012, p. 254). Also, the idea that PB in particular, and democracy in general, tries to be as inclusive as possible enters into the decision to not only allow but to encourage people to tell stories.

> To allow only rational, logical, and elaborate arguments raises the critique from some theorists that such a definition discriminates against persons with little rationalistic skill.
>
> Given the inclusionary spirit of the deliberative model, such persons should also be allowed to participate in the political process.
>
> (Steiner, 2012, p. 9)

Recall earlier in this chapter, in the 'conditions needed for public deliberation' section that if the group size is too large it can impede the quality of discussions. It was recommended that working groups should have between four to ten people (Talpin, 2011). Also in this chapter, in the 'recommendations for communicative dimension' section it noted that the composition of working, such as gender, level of education, marginalized groups, and language skills, is critical to encourage deliberation. And the role of facilitators in working groups is also critical.

Thus, it is recommended that initially the evaluation of the quality of deliberation is focused in the working groups because most of the deliberation should be occurring there. And it will help with evaluating what effect the composition of the group has on deliberation as well as the role of the facilitator. Also, any lessons learned from the working groups should transfer to the large public forums.

It is recommended that the method used to evaluate working group deliberations is the Deliberative Transformative Moments (DTM). It was developed in a paper written in 2014.

> We [Jaramillo & Steiner] want to know how long a discussion stays at a high level of deliberation, when it is transformed to a low level, how long it

How Can the Hypothesis Be Tested? 69

stays at this low level, and when it is transformed back to a high level. Theoretically, the key question for us is to identify the group dynamic context that leads to upward and downward Deliberative Transformative Moments (DTM).

(Jaramillo & Steiner, 2014, p. 2)

It was designed to catch the quick back and forth of small group discussions.

Obviously, the coding is critical to determine the comparative quality of deliberation. Jaramillo and Steiner wrote the following.

The analysts should have audio- and video recordings and the respective transcripts of the group discussions at their disposal. To come to a good classification decision, the analyst should take their time and consult these tapes and transcripts time and again to get a sense for the context in which a speech act is uttered.

(2014, p. 3)

Measuring the quality of deliberation is needed so the findings can be discussed with PBNYC researchers, facilitators, and participants in order to make adjustments to improve the deliberation. They are looking for turning points where an individual speech act started or ended high quality deliberation within the group. This information can be used for training purposes.

As noted at the beginning of this section, analysts need to be open to changing the ways they measure the quality of deliberation. Just as the facilitators need to constantly looking for ways to improve deliberation, the research analysts need to be constantly trying to improve their measurements by talking to the facilitators and participants.

Each speech act is assigned to one of four categories. The first one is that the level of deliberation remains high.

Our criterion is whether the discussion continues to *flow* in an interactive way on a particular topic with the actors listening to each other with respect. Deliberation also stays high if an actor introduces another topic, giving reasons why the topic is linked with the issue assigned to the group.

(Jaramillo & Steiner, 2014, p. 2)

The second category is when the level of deliberation transforms from high to low. "We [Jaramillo & Steiner] use this second category when the *flow* of the discussion is *disrupted*" (Jaramillo & Steiner, 2014, p. 2). The third category is when the level of deliberation remains at a low level. "The speaker is unable or unwilling to put on the agenda a topic relevant for the issue that the group is expected to discuss" (Jaramillo & Steiner, 2014, p. 3). And the fourth category is when the level of deliberation is transformed from a low level to a high level of deliberation. "Speech acts according to the fourth category are successful in formulating a new topic relevant for the issue assigned to the group" (Jaramillo

70 *How Can the Hypothesis Be Tested?*

& Steiner, 2014, p. 3). Obviously, the analysts will need to know the context of the speech to know whether it was a turning point.

The only thing left to measure are the four intangible benefits in the hypothesis. The participant questionnaire is pretty straightforward. Of course, a short definition of public happiness is needed before people are asked how often they experience it. Answers to all five questions are five-point scales ranging from never to always.

There are two questions about morality which are not as straightforward. It has been found that framing an issue as moral cause people to become defensive. "Thinking about an issue as moral not only heightens resistance to persuasion, but also lessens people's receptiveness to the views of those close to them" (Bloom & Levitan, 2011, p. 659). Thus, instead of asking about how often participants are caused to reflect on morality, they are asked about "social justice (human rights and equality)". The same terminology is used when asking how often they change their views on these issues.

This research indicates that how a facilitator frames an issue for discussion matters.

> Results demonstrate that morality and network composition interact to predict persuasion, such that when people are not cued to consider morality increased network heterogeneity predicts increased persuasion, but when identical messages are presented in a way that involves morality the impact of network heterogeneity disappears or even reverses marginally.
>
> (Bloom & Levitan, 2011, p. 643)

Thus, this information should be part of the deliberation training.

And since all of the recommended changes may take time to put in place, it would necessary to measure the degree to which the recommendations have been implemented in order to measure the impact these changes have on the hypothesis, as they are implemented. This should help researchers determine whether additional adjustments need to be made. The measurements should start before the changes are implemented and continue after all recommendations are in place. This continuous evaluation of PB will help guard against Dewey's unintended consequences.

Notes

1 For further documentation, see Chapter 1's evaluation of Porto Alegre's PB.
2 See extensive literature about proposed Job Guarantee Program by Wray, Forstater, and others.

References

Abdullah, C., Karpowitz, C., & Raphael, C. (2016). Affinity groups, enclave deliberation, and equity. *Journal of Public Deliberation, 12*(2 Special Issue), article 6.

How Can the Hypothesis Be Tested? 71

Appadurai, A. (2004). The capacity to aspire: Culture and the terms of recognition. In V. Rao & M. Walton (Eds.), *Culture and public action* (pp. 59–84). Stanford, CA: Stanford University Press.

Baiocchi, G. (2003). Emergent public spheres: Talking politics in participatory governance. *American Sociological Review, 68*(1), 52–74.

Baiocchi, G., & Ganuza, E. (2017). *Popular democracy: The paradox of participation.* Stanford, CA: Stanford University Press.

Bloom, P., & Levitan, L. (2011). We're closer than I thought: Social network heterogeneity, morality, and political persuasion. *Political Psychology, 32*(4), 643–665.

Community Development Project. (2015). A research and evaluation report on participatory budgeting in New York City, PB Cycle 4 (2014–15). Retrieved from https://cdp. urbanjustice.org/sites/default/files/CDP.WEB.doc_Report_PBNYC_cycle4find ings_20151021.pdf

Dewey, J. (1954). *The public and its problems.* Athens, OH: Swallow Press/Ohio University Press Books.

Gilman, H. (2012). Transformative deliberations: Participatory budgeting in the United States. *Journal of Public Deliberation, 8*(2), article 11.

Heller, P., & Rao, V. (2015). Deliberation and development. In P. Heller & V. Rao (Eds.), *Deliberation and development* (pp. 1–23). Washington, DC: World Bank Group.

Hayduk, R., Hackett, K., & Folla, D. (2017). Immigrant engagement in participatory budgeting in New York City. *New Political Science, 39*(1), 76–94.

Jabola-Carolus, I. (2017). Growing grassroots democracy: Dynamic outcomes in building New York City's participatory budgeting program. *New Political Science, 39*(1), 109–125.

Jaramillo, M., & Steiner, J. (2014). Deliberative transformative moments: A new concept as amendment to the discourse quality index. *Journal of Public Deliberation, 10*(2), article 8.

Leighninger, M., & Rinehart, C. (2016). Power to the people! (and settings for using it wisely?): Balancing direct and deliberative democracy in participatory budgeting. *Public Agenda.* Retrieved from www.publicagenda.org/files/PowertothePeople_Public Agenda_2016.pdf

Lerner, J., & Pape, M. (2016). Budgeting for equity: How can participatory budgeting advance equity in the United States? *Journal of Public Deliberation, 12*(2 Special Issue), article 9.

Lerner, J., & Secondo, D. (2012). By the people, for the people: Participatory budgeting from the bottom up in North America. *Journal of Public Deliberation, 8*(2), article 2.

Moscrop, D., & Warren, M. (2016). When is deliberation democratic? *Journal of Public Deliberation, 12*(2 Special Issue), article 4.

New York City Council. (2018). *Participatory budgeting: Volunteer.* https://council.nyc. gov/pb/participate/

Participatory Budgeting Project. (2017a). *Budget delegate guide.* Retrieved from https:// council.nyc.gov/pb/resources-for-budget-delegates-and-facilitators/

Participatory Budgeting Project. (2017b). *Idea ranking tool.* Retrieved from https:// council.nyc.gov/pb/resources-for-budget-delegates-and-facilitators/

Pateman, C. (2012). Participatory democracy revisited. *American Political Science Association, 10*(1), 7–19.

Steiner, J. (2012). *The foundations of deliberative democracy: Empirical research and normative implications.* Cambridge, UK: Cambridge University Press.

Su, C. (2017). From Porto Alegre to New York City: Participatory budgeting and democracy. *New Political Science, 39*(1), 67–75.

72 *How Can the Hypothesis Be Tested?*

Talpin, J. (2011). *Schools of democracy*. UK: European Consortium for Political Research.

Thompson, D. (2008). Deliberative democratic theory and empirical political science. *Annual Review of Political Science, 11*, 497–520. doi: 10.1146/annurev.polisci.11.081306.070555

Wampler, B. (2007). A guide to participatory budgeting. In A. Shah (Ed.), *Participatory budgeting* (pp. 21–53). Washington, DC: The World Bank.

Wampler, B. (2012). Participatory budgeting: Core principles and key impacts. *Journal of Public Deliberation, 8*(2), article 12.

4 Public Happiness

One of the potential benefits of PB is an increased sense of public happiness. This social phenomenon is said to occur in individuals who devote time and energy to help govern their local community. In other words, people experience joy from helping to ensure that local governments function well. This social phenomenon is explored by examining Thomas Jefferson's proposal for a ward system. He felt it would revitalize our system of representative government by helping citizens pursue public happiness and would reinvigorate people through their participation in local government. Basically, it is a proposal for local direct democracy throughout the United States. Jefferson was a great thinker with a wide variety of interests and viewpoints. His political philosophy concerning participation was very progressive. His ideas about participation are the subject of this chapter.

First, it is interesting to note Walt Whitman's view of happiness. In the 1855 preface to "Leaves of Grass," Whitman wrote, "For the eternal tendencies of all toward happiness make the only point of sane philosophy" (1982, p. 18). Increased public happiness is an important reason for the suggested changes in PB's rules, practices, and procedures (Chapter 3), as well as the institutional adjustment (Chapter 2) suggested to free PBNYC from arbitrary rulings of city agencies.

Another social philosopher, Robert Putnam, saw the connection between happiness and the degree to which people are involved in their communities. Putnam found a correlation between happiness and our number of social connections. Although he did hedge his bet when he wrote,

> [T]he direction of causation remains ambiguous. Perhaps happy people are more likely than unlikely than unhappy people to get married, win raises at work, continue in school, attend church, join clubs, host parties, and so on. My present purpose is merely to illustrate that social connections have profound links with psychological well-being. The Beatles got it right: we all "get by with a little help from our friends."
>
> (2000, p. 334)

Social phenomena are difficult to empirically measure because they are intertwined and as Dewey noted they are impossible to isolate for the purpose of

74 *Public Happiness*

study. However, Jefferson was a visionary and seemed to understand public happiness.

Thomas Jefferson is best known for being the author of the Declaration of Independence. Of course, he was also the third President of the United States. After he left office, Jefferson proposed in letters to various people that a ward system be created in the United States. Each ward would be small enough so every resident could meet in town hall-type meetings to decide community issues. Each ward would be like a little republic which would maintain the roads, run the schools, be responsible for police protection, and take care of the poor (Jefferson, 2011). Jefferson wrote, "I am not among those who fear the people. They, and not the rich, are our dependence for continued freedom" (Jefferson, 2011, p. 1400). Jefferson felt that putting faith in the people was the best way to guarantee our freedoms. In Jefferson's vision, everyone would become an acting member of the government.

The ward-republics seem to be patterned both on the New England townships and on the American Indians' tribal councils (Matthews, 1986). Jefferson was an admirer of American Indians and their way of life. And in a letter to Joseph Cabell, he acknowledged the power of the New England townships concerning their opposition to an embargo. Jefferson wrote, "I felt the foundations of the government shaken under my feet by the New England townships" (Jefferson, 2011, p. 1381). Jefferson knew from prior experience with New England townships that the proposed ward system would have great political power, and he knew that the tribal councils worked well for the American Indians.

Another more recent example of the moral power of New England townships is from the 1980s.

> [T]he nuclear freeze resolution that was adopted by more than a hundred town meetings in Vermont, ... [in 1980s] ... leading to ad hoc "town meetings" in regions of the country that had never seen them, it affected national policy on this issue and culminated in a demonstration of approximately a million people in New York City.
>
> (Bookchin, 1995, p. 230)

Obviously, the New England townships were not empowered to have anything to do with federal policy. But they have been a vehicle for the people to express their opinion to elected politicians.

Jefferson studied how American Indians interacted with each other, including how they governed themselves. "Their [American Indians] only controls are their manners, and that moral sense of right and wrong, which, like the sense of tasting and feeling, in every man makes a part of his nature" (Jefferson, 2011, p. 220). Jefferson admired the way that American Indian tribes were able to live in peace and without coercive government, which was more than the civilized Europeans had achieved (Jefferson, 2011). Within each tribe and within each confederation, the American Indians lived in peace.

Of course, there were Indian wars between confederations and between tribes that were not part of the same confederation. "Indian wars were usually begun

Public Happiness   75

for defense or revenge. Because of the common practice of *blood revenge*, it was hard to end a war" (Barrett, 1946, p. 111). The blood revenge custom made it practically impossible to stop an Indian war, after it began.

> These frequent wars were the cause which brought into use the Indian Confederacies and Leagues of Nation, such as the Iroquois League in the northeastern United States, the Creek Confederacy in the southeast, [and] the Sioux or Dakota Confederacy in the middle west.
>
> (Barrett, 1946, p. 116)

Sometimes these confederations would expand to include additional tribes.

The other type of Indian war were the wars between American Indians and European settlers.

> After European settlers came wars between the Indian tribes gradually grew less frequent until they may be considered a thing of the past, but wars between Indians and whites multiplied during the post-Columbian period [after Columbus discovered America]. Foremost among the causes of wars with Indians was the seizing of lands by the white colonists.
>
> (Barrett, 1946, p. 117)

It is not clear if the reduced warfare among Indian tribes was due to increased confederation activity, or if the reduced warfare among Indian tribes was due to the greater danger of the European settlers. Perhaps both had the effect of reducing warfare among the Indian tribes.

In part, it seems tribal society may have been a model for the ward system. Jefferson did not believe that coercive government was needed to force people to live together in peace. "Jefferson bases his theory on sociability, not on individuality" (Matthews, 1986, p. 64). Tradition, custom, friendship, and clans allowed American Indians to live in peace within confederations of tribes. Everyone had a say in Indian tribes, which were ruled by consensus.

Jefferson conceived of ward-republics to give everyone a voice in government. This was an innovative and original idea for combining local direct democracy with representative democracy. Through the system of wards, the government would be assured of keeping in touch with the concerns and the needs of the people. The people who live in the community are best qualified to govern the community (Jefferson, 2011). In addition to providing the best possible local governance, the ward-republics would continuously be providing experience and training that people could use to interact with or serve in the county, state, or federal government. This system would help train people to be good citizens in our representative government by providing a space where they would engage in debating and compromising.

Jefferson believed the best way to protect our rights was to obtain the greatest degree of popular participation (Jefferson, 2011). "Through daily action in the ward-republics, then, Jefferson thinks he has found a permanent check to

76 *Public Happiness*

tyranny" (Matthews, 1986, p. 87). Jefferson had complete faith in the people, as a whole, to follow their conscience and do the right thing. In an 1819 letter to Spencer Roane, Jefferson wrote: "Independence can be trusted nowhere but with the people in mass. They are inherently independent of all but moral law" (2011, p. 1426). Because Jefferson had a very positive view of human nature, he believed local direct democracy would work.

Jefferson's proposal is a great idea. The question is, has anyone tried it? Arendt has noted that most modern revolutions have seemed to naturally create an environment where local direct democracies, or as she says councils, have appeared. She did not provide a detailed model for council democracy (Sitton, 1987).

> Her [Arendt's] purpose instead is simply to sketch a political structure to illustrate the possibility of realizing alternative political principles; direct democracy, the experience of public freedom and public happiness in the modern world, an arena for proper opinion formation.
>
> (Sitton, 1987, p. 82)

Arendt saw, and wrote about, the values of local direct democracies.

Arendt wrote; "[N]o tradition, either revolutionary or pre-revolutionary, can be called to account for the regular emergence, and reemergence of the council system ever since the French Revolution" (2006, p. 253). The author goes on to list several examples.

> [T]he year 1870, when the French capital under siege by the Prussian army ... formed the nucleus for the Parisian Commune government in the spring of 1871; the year 1905, ... outside all revolutionary parties and groups, and the workers in the factories organized themselves into councils, *soviets*...; the years 1918 and 1919 in Germany, when, after the defeat of the army, soldiers and workers in open rebellion constituted themselves into *Arbeiter-* and *Soldatenräte* ... in Munich in the spring of 1919, the short-lived Bavarian *Räterepublick*; the last date, finally, is the autumn of 1956, ... the Hungarian Revolution, in Budapest.
>
> (Arendt, 2006, p. 254)

The functionality and value of these local councils must have been apparent to modern revolutionaries.

Why then has this form of local governance not survived and grown? Ardent saw a fundamental conflict between the councils and the political parties. "The conflict between the two systems, the parties and the councils, came to the fore in all twentieth-century revolutions. The issue at stake was representation verses action and participation" (Arendt, 2006, p. 265). The councils were best at action and participation. After the revolutions were over, it was thought that management and administration were more important. "They agreed ... that the substance of politics was not action but administration" (Arendt, 2006, p. 265).

Public Happiness 77

However, this and later chapters show that both action and participation are needed to experience public happiness, increase understanding of others, develop individuals' and communities' morality, and create a sense of belonging. Working together to help one another helps to reduce preconceived stereotypes and leads to understanding of others. An empowered people will work to make the right decisions for themselves, their families, and their communities leading to public happiness.

Perhaps a middle way between direct democracy and political parties would be the best approach. Such as implementing local direct democracies while keeping representative democracy, with political parties, at the higher levels as proposed by Jefferson. The action and participation at the local level could act as a counter-balance to the power of the political parties by their ability to call people to action. Of course, these public assemblies would only have legislative power for local issues. But they could also pass nonbinding resolutions, as noted earlier.

Jefferson incorporated the notion of local direct democracy with modern representative government.

> His species of republicanism must be identified with a pyramid, starting from wards, nestled directly in the midst of the people, to counties, states, and the central Federal Government. The democratic impulse, starting with its home-made lessons in the "pure republics" at the base, travels up the various levels of the pyramid, its strength at each successive level depending upon the purity and force of the original impulse.
>
> (Koch, 1964, p. 164)

The mass of people at the base is the force that drives the system. Participants would feel reinvigorated with their experience of becoming the local government. Most likely, many would also get involved in higher levels of government, which would revitalize those governments. The desire to participate, the desire for social interaction, and the desire for public happiness are what would inspire the mass of people.

Public happiness seems to be what motivated Jefferson to promote this ward system proposal. Jefferson's choice of "pursuit of happiness," in the Declaration of Independence, is interesting because he did not specify if he meant private happiness or public happiness. It seems reasonable to conclude that he meant both.

> This freedom they called later, when they had come to taste it, "public happiness," and it consisted in the citizen's right of access to the public realm, in his share in public power – to be "a participator in the government of affairs" in Jefferson's telling phase [2011, p. 1380] – as distinct from the generally recognized rights of subjects to be protected by the government in the pursuit of private happiness even against public power.
>
> (Arendt, 2006, p. 118)

78 *Public Happiness*

In order to experience public happiness, people need to live up to their potential of being fully engaged in their communities. This includes being actively involved with their neighbors in governing their own communities to be able to achieve public happiness.

If individuals do not exercise their right to public happiness and publicly participate in government, they become powerless and must be protected from the potential misuse of public power.

> It [freedom] resides no longer in the public realm but in the private life of the citizens and so must be defended against the public and its power. Freedom and power have parted company, and the fateful equating of power with violence, of the political with government, and of government with a necessary evil has begun.
>
> (Arendt, 2006, p. 128)

Giving up our right to public happiness by not participating creates a government that we must be protected from. By default, government must take up the slack by relying on its monopoly on violence to enforce its actions. The political parties and politicians take the power that was not claimed by the people. Inaction of the people results in their loss of public happiness, loss of power, and the creation of a government that the people must be protected from.

> Government need not be a necessary evil which must be endured. Through public participation the people reclaim their power and freedom from coercive government. By becoming active in governing their communities the people become the government. Through the mouth of Theseus, the legendary founder of Athens and hence her spokesman, what it was that enabled ordinary men, young and old, to bear life's burden; it was the polis, the space of men's free deeds and living words, which could, endow life with splendor.
>
> (Arendt, 2006, p. 173)

Most importantly, public participation fills a need we have to be socially active.

The pursuit of happiness is the basis of Jefferson's ward system because it would guarantee a space where people could pursue public happiness through their participation in their community.

> The basic assumption of the ward system, whether Jefferson knew it or not, was that no one could be called happy without his share in public happiness, that no one could be called free without his experience in public freedom, and no one could be called either happy or free without participating, and having a share, in public power.
>
> (Arendt, 2006, p. 247)

The ward system was meant to provide the means for the people to fulfill their desires for happiness and freedom. At the same time, it would create a much stronger nation that was much more flexible and responsive to the people.

By creating a public space where everyone could deliberate, the ward system would maintain the spirit of revolution. In a letter to James Madison in January 1787, Jefferson wrote, "I hold that a little rebellion now and then is a good thing, and as necessary in the political world as storms in the physical....It is a medicine necessary for the sound health of government" (2011, p. 882). Revolution is a time when everything is re-examined. Old ideas can be swept aside to make room for new innovative solutions.

The fact that revolutions do not create institutions to perpetuate the revolutionary spirit is a paradox. The goal of revolutions has been to create a new concrete and permanent foundation for society. And the revolutionary spirit is by definition constantly changing and evolving. It is ironic that freedom is the price paid for the foundation (Arendt, 2006). Jefferson proposed the ward system because he perceived "that the Revolution, while it had given freedom to the people, had failed to provide a space where this freedom could be exercised" (Arendt, 2006, p. 227). A truly successful revolution would make the revolution permanent, without continuous violence, by creating space where the people could exercise their freedom. The founders, other than Jefferson, may have taken the revolutionary spirit for granted.

> It was precisely because of the enormous weight of the Constitution and of the experiences in founding a new body that the failure to incorporate the townships and the town-hall meetings, the original springs of all political activity in country, amounted to a death sentence for them. Paradoxical as it may sound, it was in fact under the impact of the Revolution that the revolutionary spirit in America began to wither away, and it was the Constitution itself, this greatest achievement of the American people, which eventually cheated them of their proudest possession.
>
> (Arendt, 2006, p. 231)

The Constitution failed to create the most important thing – a space for the participation of the people that would help ensure their freedom and happiness.

An empowered and deliberative PB process gives people a space where they can engage in public deliberations, and make decisions about community issues. An expanded PB process would allow residents to become the local government. Thus, PB has the potential to increase public happiness, rekindle the American spirit, and inspire people to get involved in higher levels of government.

References

Arendt, H. (2006). *On revolution* (4th ed.). New York: Penguin Books.
Barrett, S. M. (1946). *Sociology of the American Indians*. Kansas City, MO: Burton Publishing.

80 *Public Happiness*

Bookchin, M. (1995). *From urbanization to cities: Toward a new politics of citizenship* (2nd ed.). London: Cassell.

Jefferson, T. (2011). *Jefferson writings* (M. Peterson, Ed.). New York: Penguin Group.

Koch, A. (1964). *The philosophy of Thomas Jefferson* (2nd ed.). Chicago, IL: Quadrangle Books.

Matthews, R. (1986). *The radical politics of Thomas Jefferson: A revisionist view* (2nd ed.). Lawrence, KS: University Press of Kansas.

Putnam, R. (2000). *Bowling alone*. New York: Simon & Schuster Paperbacks.

Sitton, J. (1987). Hannah Arendt's argument for council democracy. *Polity, 20*(1), 80–100.

Whitman, W. (1982). *Whitman: Poetry and prose*. New York: The Library of America.

5 Increased Understanding of Others

This chapter explores the recent philosophical history of gaining a better understanding of others, which is one of the potential benefits of PB. This chapter helps one develop a better perception of why understanding others is important, why it may be difficult, and how it may be possible. A better understanding of this potential benefit will help to design ways that PB's rules, procedures, and practices could be changed to better promote understanding of others.

The first section briefly reviews why Dewey believes understanding of others is important. The next section looks at Mills' reasoning as to why modern society has made understanding of others more difficult and his solution. The last section examines Schutz's phenomenological research, which explains how people can understand each other and its implications for dealing with racism.

John Dewey

To understand Dewey's work better, it will help to gain a better comprehension of Dewey's worldview. Dewey wrote, "Progress means increase of present meaning, which involves multiplication of sensed distinctions as well as harmony, unification" (2002, p. 283). Dewey realized that we are all social beings, and thus social interaction is what has meaning and how we define our progress.

During social interactions we can acknowledge our differences as well as acknowledging how we are really the same, and in harmony with one another. "An activity has meaning in the degree in which it establishes and acknowledges variety and intimacy of connections" (Dewey, 2002, p. 293). The quality of our relationships is determined by the degree of their familiarity and closeness while recognizing our differences. "Without openhearted dialogue, the human spirit stops growing and withers away. Without intellectual and spiritual exchange, society rigidifies and grinds to a halt. Dewey clearly pointed out the path to the unfettered development of humanity and society" (Ikeda, as cited in Garrison et al. 2014, p. 1). Honest communication among people searching for common ground is what gives meaning to life.

82   *Increased Understanding of Others*

This communication is also what enables people to understand one another.

> In a word, that expansion and reënforcement of personal understanding and judgment by the cumulative and transmitted wealth of the community which may render nugatory the indictment of democracy drawn on the basis of the ignorance, bias and levity of the masses, can be fulfilled only in the relations of personal intercourse in the local community.
>
> (Dewey, 1954, p. 218)

Personal communication not only promotes understanding among people, it also can improve judgment.

On the other hand, lack of open and honest communication in a community invites intolerance. "An anti-humanist attitude is the essence of every form of intolerance" (Dewey, 1993a, p. 227). Communication reminds us that we are all the same; we are all human beings.

> Intolerance, abuse, calling of names because of differences of opinion about religion or politics or business, as well as because of differences of race, color, wealth or degree of culture are treason to the democratic way of life. For everything which bars freedom and fullness of communication sets up barriers that divide human beings into sets and cliques, into antagonistic sects and factions, and thereby undermines the democratic way of life.
>
> (Dewey, 1993b, p. 243)

Ongoing discussions with everyone in the community is the antidote for intolerance. "Dewey was convinced that the local, face-to-face community is necessary to form and sustain any public" (Garrison et al., 2014, p. 160). Face-to-face communication tends to break down barriers between people.

PB facilitators can encourage a wide diversity of people to communicate with each other. And public deliberation provides a framework of civility, which facilitators can enforce, until it becomes apparent to participants that basically we are all the same, in spite of our differences, and that everyone deserves to be treated with dignity and respect. Ongoing discussions and deliberations within the community are a necessity and constitute part of Dewey's "proper conditions" for democracy to flourish.

C. Wright Mills

Mills was a sociologist who published most of his work in the 1950s and addressed the big structural changes taking place in the country. "Mills admired what he called the 'classic tradition' of social science. In that tradition the questions asked are generally of a wide scope, concern total societies and the studies are 'soaked in history'" (Sigler, 1966, p. 32). Many of Mills' ideas were outside of mainstream thought. "C. Wright Mills was an academic gadfly whose writings served as both an inspiration and an irritant to a whole generation of social

Increased Understanding of Others 83

scientists" (Sigler, 1966, p. 32). Many of Mills' ideas related directly or indirectly to political science. He was a strong proponent of democracy.

Mills' understanding was that since many people do not understand the structure of modern society it affects their ability to reason about it. This leads to feelings of powerlessness for the ordinary citizen and feelings of alienation for the workers in bureaucracies. As Mills wrote, in *The Sociological Imagination*,

> Great and rational organizations – in brief, bureaucracies – have indeed increased, but the substantive reason of the individual has not. Caught in the limited milieu of their everyday lives, ordinary men often cannot reason about the great structures – rational and irrational – of which their milieu are subordinate parts.
>
> (2000a, p. 168)

Even though a bureaucracy may directly affect our lives, if it is outside of our direct experiences, we may not be able to make sense of it. Mills wrote, "The growth of such organizations, within an increasing division of labor, sets up more and more spheres of life, work, and leisure, in which reasoning is difficult or impossible" (2000a, p. 168). Thus, the trend seems to be a decreasing capacity for human reasoning and its resultant consequences.

Historically, human reasoning has been a necessary, but not sufficient, condition for human freedom. In *The Sociological Imagination*, Mills wrote that liberalism and socialism as our two major inherited orientations. "These two ideologies came out of The Enlightenment, and they have in common many assumptions and values. In both, increased rationality is held to be the prime condition of increased freedom" (2000a, p. 166). Thus, decreased capacity to reason creates a problem of freedom.

The ability to reason is fundamental for freedom and democracy to flourish.

> It is not too much to say that in the extreme development the chance to reason of most men is destroyed, as rationality increases and its locus, its control, is moved from the individual to the big-scale organization. There is then rationality without reason. Such rationality is not commensurate with freedom but the destroyer of it.
>
> (Mills, 2000a, p. 170)

When control of organizations is moved outside the scope of individuals' influence and understanding, the freedom of individuals is in jeopardy.

Mills' definition of bureaucracy went beyond governmental agencies. Mills used bureaucracy to refer to corporations as well as government agencies (Mills, 2002). He defined bureaucracy: "Descriptively, bureaucracy refers to a hierarchy of offices or bureaus, each with an assigned area of operation, each employing a staff having specialized qualifications" (2002, p. 78). Mills wrote that as corporate bureaucracies grow, government bureaucracies increase their staff in an attempt to control the corporate bureaucracies. Then the corporate bureaucracies

84   Increased Understanding of Others

respond by hiring government officials and placing their members on governmental commissions and agencies (2002). Thus, there seems to be no end to the growth of bureaucracies.

In addition to looking at the impact bureaucracies have on the ordinary citizen, Mills reasoned that the effect bureaucracies have on many of their workers is alienation. This is due to the workers not only not having a say in the bureaucracies' goals, they may not even understand why they are doing their jobs. In *The Sociological Imagination*, Mills explained the dilemma in which these workers find themselves.

> He gears his aspirations and his work to the situation he is in. In due course, he does not seek a way out; he adapts....Alienated from production, from work, he is also alienated from consumption [because consumption is also being rationalized], from genuine leisure. This adaptation of the individual and its effects upon his milieu and self results not only in the loss of his chance, and in due course, of his capacity and his will to reason; it also affects his chances and his capacity to act as a free man. Indeed, neither the value of freedom nor of reason, it would seem, are known to him.
>
> (2000a, p. 170)

The dilemma that these workers seem to face is the choice between their freedom and making a living. Mills wrote, "The society in which this [alienated] man, this cheerful robot, flourishes is the antithesis of the free society – or in the literal and plain meaning of the word, of a democratic society" (2000b, p. 172). Mills believed the distraction or influence of the mass media might be a reason that some workers do not seem to directly address this issue (1979, 2002).

Regarding mass media reporting political issues, Mills wrote in "Letter to the New Left," "Their power to outrage, their power truly to enlighten in a political way, their power to aid decision, even their power to clarify some situation – all that is blunted or destroyed" (2008, p. 256). Mills wrote that "reasoning collapses into reasonableness" (2008, p. 256). He goes on to explain that many times, "arguments and facts of a displeasing kind are simply ignored" (2008, p. 256), and when arguments and facts are acknowledged, "they are neither connected with one another nor related to any general view. Acknowledged in a scattered way, they are never put together: to do so is to risk being called, curiously enough, 'one-sided'" (2008, p. 256). Mills goes on to examine the consequences of such reporting:

> This refusal to relate isolated facts and fragmentary comment with the changing institutions of society makes it impossible to understand the structural realities which these facts might reveal; the longer-run trends of which they might be tokens. In brief, fact and idea are isolated, so the real questions are not even raised, analysis of the meanings of fact not even begun.
>
> (2008, p. 256)

Increased Understanding of Others 85

Thus, the role of the mass media contributes to the decline of our capacity to understand and to reason.

Mass media has had much to do with the emergence and maintenance of mass society. In *The Power Elite*, Mills wrote, "In a mass society, the dominant type of communication is the formal media, and the publics become mere media markets: all those exposed to the contents of given mass media" (2000b, p. 304). Mills saw a trend away from a community of publics toward a mass society.

> In the United States today, media markets are not entirely ascendant over primary publics. But surely we can see that many aspects of the public life of our times are more features of a mass society than of a community of publics.
>
> (Mills, 2000b, p. 304)

Mills used publics in much the same way as Dewey: a group of people getting together to resolve one or more community issues through public deliberation. Mills distinguished publics from masses by the type of communication taking place in each, including the degree of autonomy from institutions they had in the formation of individuals' opinions. A public forms opinion by discussion with a great deal of independence from institutions; while masses are strongly influenced by the mass media. Other distinguishing factors include the portion of people giving opinion, social action resulting from opinion, and who is allowed to speak. In general, in publics everyone is allowed to speak, and once agreement is reached, social action is likely to occur; while in masses, hardly anyone has a chance to speak and social action is less likely (Mills, 2000b, pp. 303–304).

People in a mass society are alienated because they feel powerless. Mills wrote, "Men in masses have troubles, but they are not usually aware of their true meaning and source; men in publics confront issues, and they usually come to be aware of their public terms" (2000a, p. 187). By engaging in community discussions, people increase their capacity to understand and act.

Mills reasoned that publics, where people deliberate face-to-face about real issues that affect them, are needed. Mills wrote in *The Causes of World War Three*, "It [political structure] requires not only that such a public as is projected by democratic theorists exist, but that it be the very forum within which a politics of real issues is enacted" (1958, p. 118). Mills goes on to clarify functions that these publics should perform, "And democracy certainly requires, as a fact of power, that there be free associations linking families and smaller communities and publics on the one hand with the state, the military establishment, the corporation on the other" (1958, p. 119). This linking is needed in order to enact policy in a democratically responsible manner where everyone has a voice.

In an empowered, deliberative, and expanded PB process, everyone will have a voice. They will be able to discuss and decide issues, which are important to their community. The scale of the community is understandable. Public deliberation can bring the community together by providing a space where individuals

86 *Increased Understanding of Others*

can gain understanding of each other's problems. Public policies can be translated to their effect on individual lives in the community.

One of the keys to making small publics work is that there needs to be a translation from individual problems to policy issues and vice versa. In *The Sociological Imagination*, Mills spelled out what he felt each social scientist should do, in order to help build a more democratic society.

> It is the political task of the social scientist – as of any liberal educator – continually to translate personal troubles into public issues, and public issues into the terms of their human meaning for a variety of individual.... And it is his purpose to cultivate such habits of mind among men and women who are publicly exposed to him. To secure these ends is to secure reason and individuality, and to make these the predominate values of a democratic society.
>
> (2000a, pp. 187–188)

This will help promote creation of and continued demand for small publics on issues relevant to the people.

These small publics would help people understand one another and their community, which will help them to improve their ability to reason. An empowered, deliberative, and expanded PB process could fill this need.

Alfred Schutz

Alfred Schutz was a social philosopher who used phenomenological analysis and the general sociological methodology of Max Weber to explore the social world. "The intersubjective world of daily life, our social world, is the domain of action, and the analysis of action is a central theme of Schutz's Phenomenology" (Natanson, 1968, p. 221).

> He [Schutz] accepts Weber's axiom that the social sciences must be value-free. He likewise accepts Weber's methodological individualism, and his contention that social phenomena are properly to be understood in terms of ideal types. And he not only accepts but emphasizes Weber's view that the social sciences are concerned essentially with social action, the concept "social" being defined in terms of a relationship between the behavior of two or more people, and the concept "action" being defined as behavior to which a subjective meaning is attached.
>
> (Walsh, 1967, p. xxi)

However, Schutz went beyond Weber's work by looking closely at the definitions of some fundamental concepts.

> Suffice it to say that, while agreeing with Weber that it is the essential function of social science to be interpretive, that is, to understand the subjective

Increased Understanding of Others 87

meaning of social action, Schutz finds that Weber failed to state clearly the essential characteristics of understanding (Verstehen), of subjective meaning (gemeinter Sinn), or of action (Handeln).

(Walsh, 1967, p. xxi)

Schutz spent his career gaining a better understanding of the subjective point of view, which gives meaning to social action. The subjective point of view is a genuine understanding of the other person's point of view. Schutz believed it was possible to achieve a perception of another's subjective experiences (Walsh, 1967). As Walsh writes in the introduction to *The Phenomenology of the Social World,*

> This does not mean that we can directly intuit another person's subjective experiences. What it does mean is that we can intentionally grasp those experiences because we assume that his facial expressions and his gestures are a "field of expression" for his inner life. This is what Schutz calls the "bodily presence" or "corporeal givenness" of the partner. The crucial factor here is simultaneity. We sense the other person's stream of consciousness is flowing along a track that is temporally parallel with our own.
>
> (p. xxv)

This allows us to gain an understanding of social action, which is needed to understand the social world.

For most of his career Schutz agreed with Weber, who limited the purpose of philosophy to value clarification as opposed to the discovery of value, and did not apply value judgments to social science (Barber, 2004). However, Schutz did come to embrace a normative stance. After the 1954 Brown vs. Board of Education of Topeka Supreme Court case, which ended the doctrine of separate but equal, Schutz attended two conferences on equality and equality of opportunity.

The first conference, in 1955, was the Conference on Science, Philosophy, and Religion, which had the topic of equality. Schutz presented the paper: Equality and the Meaning Structure of the Social World. "Schutz's endeavor to disclose the hidden subjectivity of the Other makes for good social science, but in the equality essay it also is an ally in the ethical struggle against racism" (Barber, 1991, p. 135). Schutz used his methodology to analyze what constitutes discrimination. The first sentence of Schutz's paper on equality states, "The subject of the present paper is the theoretical analysis of various aspects of the notion of equality in the common-sense thinking of concrete social groups" (1976, p. 226). Schutz looked at the reasons why people treated others in their community as they did.

In this equality paper, Schutz starts to move away from his belief that value judgments should not be applied to social science research. "In "Equality and the Meaning Structure of the Social World," Schutz employs terms laden with moral connotations such as "degradation," "oppression," "alienation," and "deprivation of rights" (Barber, 1991, p. 134). Evidently, Schutz felt that some human action,

88 *Increased Understanding of Others*

such as discrimination, is immoral. In "Equality and the Meaning Structure of the Social World," Schutz writes:

> But if he [anyone] is compelled to identify himself as a whole with that particular trait or characteristic which places him in terms of the imposed system of heterogeneous relevances into a social category he had never included as a relevant one in his definition of his private situation, then he feels that he is no longer treated as a human being in his own right and freedom, but is degraded to an interchangeable specimen of the typified class. He is alienated from himself, a mere representative of the typified traits and characteristics. He is deprived of his right to the pursuit of happiness.
>
> (1976, pp. 256–257)

If the typifications of the in-group become internalized into the subjective viewpoints of individuals who are part of the out-group, then discrimination, with disastrous consequences, will occur (Schutz, 1976). Lack of communication results in people not knowing or not caring how their attitudes affect others. In "Making Music Together," Schutz wrote about "the "mutual tuning-in relationship" upon which alone all communication is founded" (1951, p. 79). To the degree that we still have discrimination is the degree to which we do not understand the need to "tune-in" with others.

In 1956, Schutz attended a follow-up conference (Embree, 1999) at the Institute of Ethics with the topic "equality of opportunity and the various barriers to it." Schutz was assigned to a committee to discuss "barriers to equality of opportunity for the development of powers of social and civic judgement" (Barber, 2004). After two weeks of discussion, Lasswell and Schutz prepared a written report of the committee's findings on June 14, 1956, which was slightly revised on July 5, 1956. Schutz said:

> Therefore, what we call barriers – and call [them] whatever you please – they are of three different types: There are, first of all, barriers as to the free flux of information; we have, secondly, barriers as to the free formation of motivations; and we have the third barrier, that the individual citizen, himself, might at least be heard as a competent authority to make the decisions or, if possible, to influence others in the sense of this decision.
>
> (Schutz, as cited in Embree, 1999, p. 273)

Of course, good information is needed for good judgment. Also, in "The Well-Informed Citizen," Schutz wrote, "It is the duty and privilege, therefore, of the well-informed citizen in a democratic society to make his private opinion prevail over the public opinion of the man on the street" (1946, p. 478). This because a well-informed opinion is more valuable. In a June 7, 1956 memorandum Schutz wrote to Lasswell, Schutz went further when he wrote:

Increased Understanding of Others 89

(6) Means for reaching this goal:

(a) Encouraging of debating clubs on all levels of education, using pro and con teams.
(b) Preparing of a list of books containing the reliable information in various fields and presenting as far as possible the various aspects of the problems involved in an objective way (these are not the "100 great books").
(c) Adult education on various levels.
(d) Non-partisan round-table conferences.
(e) Sponsoring inter-professional, inter-confessional, inter-racial, etc. discussion groups.
(f) Sponsoring television programs to this purpose.

(1999, pp. 294–295)

At least three of Schutz's recommendations involved public deliberations. Another two, television programs and adult education, could include deliberation.

Schutz's second type of barrier was free formation of motivations. "Schutz has an account of reasonableness, which also relates to the question of the well-informed citizen's insight into her motives" (Embree, 1999, p. 278). Schutz wrote,

If an actor seems to be sensible to the observer and is, in addition, supposed to spring from a judicious choice among different courses of action, we may call it reasonable even if such action follows traditional or habitual patterns just taken for granted. Rational action, however, presupposes that the actor has clear and distinct insight ... into the ends, the means, and the secondary results.

(Embree, 1999, p. 278)

Social policies are complex in that they may not result in the intended consequences, or they may result in additional unforeseen consequences.[1] Also, a person's motivation might be partially, or wholly, based on a biased opinion.

The third barrier, as identified by Schutz, to equality of opportunity for the development of powers of social and civic judgment was the opportunity for the individual citizen to be heard, make decisions, and influence others. In a draft of a section of the Schutz-Lasswell committee report, Schutz wrote,

(c) Barriers of equality of opportunity of bringing about the alternative chosen by the individual or at least being heard by those who make the decision.

... The social world has several dimensions in time: contemporaries, predecessors, and successors. We are here concerned exclusively with the world

90   *Increased Understanding of Others*

of contemporaries. It consists in a kernel of situations in which the individuals participate in what might be called a face-to-face relationship in the sense that the participants share a sector of space and live together [during] a stretch of time....

In the group of consocii (family, congregation, local town hall meeting, local professional group) the individual may talk to individuals, answer questions in immediacy, argue in vivid discussion. He has at least theoretically an opportunity to be heard equal to all others....

The only hope for a remedy consists in the assumption that by speaking out among the familiar group of consocii a kind of chain reaction can be created which might bring about the desired result. By the very reason of the activity of the responsible citizen in the smallest circle accessible to him – the family, the classroom, the discussion group, the local political or professional organization – is of the highest importance and should be encouraged.

(Embree, 1999, pp. 269–271)

"In this fragment on being heard, he [Schutz] went even further by discerning within intersubjective knowledge formation an ethical value of ultimacy: the single individual wishing to make his personal opinion heard and appreciated" (Barber, 2004, p. 192). Schutz discovered the ethical value of a citizen's ability to be heard and influence others as a way to judge democracy.

The PB process could overcome all three "barriers to equality of opportunity for the development of powers of social and civic judgment" which were summarized by Schutz. The well run PB process provides citizens with sufficient information to make informed decisions concerning their communities. Chapter 3 recommends changes in PB's rules, procedures, and practices to encourage deliberation, which will further help participants become better informed. Schutz's second point concerns an individual's motivation for his judgment. Schutz was referring to "the ends, the means, and the secondary results." These concerns are explained by Dewey's explanation of the means-end continuum and unintended consequences (see Chapter 2), which are mitigated by the measurement proposed in Chapter 3. The other barrier that might result from a person's motivation was that the motivation might be based on a biased opinion. This is addressed by facilitators encouraging deliberation, which should help expose any bias. And finally, the PB assemblies give every citizen the chance to stand up and be heard concerning issues affecting their local communities. And since the PB process is open and transparent, every citizen will know the outcome of every issue that was raised during the process.

A well-run PB process can promote understanding of others, per Schutz's research of face-to-face interactions. It seems logical that PB would tend to reduce discrimination, especially if public deliberation is a goal, because in order for people to be able to deliberate they need to deliberate as equals (Heller &

Rao, 2015). As explained earlier, PB can help overcome Schutz's three barriers to equality of opportunity by providing space where participants can increase their understanding of each other while increasing their understanding of community.

Note

1 See Chapter 2 for Dewey's explanation of the means-end-continuum and unintended consequences.

References

Barber, M. (1991). The ethics behind the absence of ethics in Alfred Schutz's thought. *Human Studies, 14*(2/3), 129–140.

Barber, M. (2004). *The participating citizen.* Albany, NY: State University of New York Press.

Dewey, J. (1954). *The public and its problems.* Athens, OH: Swallow Press/Ohio University Press Books.

Dewey, J. (1993a). The need for a recovery of philosophy. In D. Morris & I. Shapiro (Eds.), *John Dewey: The political writings* (pp. 1–9). Indianapolis, IN: Hackett Publishing Company.

Dewey, J. (1993b). Creative democracy: The task before us. In D. Morris & I. Shapiro (Eds.), *John Dewey: The political writings* (pp. 240–245). Indianapolis, IN: Hackett Publishing Company.

Dewey, J. (2002). *Human nature and conduct* (2nd ed.). Toronto, Canada: General Publishing Company.

Embree, L. (1999). The ethical-political side of Schutz: His contributions at the 1956 Institute on Ethics concerned with barriers to equality of opportunity. In L. Embree (Ed.), *Schutzian social science* (pp. 235–285). Dordrecht, The Netherlands: Kluwer Academic Publishers.

Garrison, J., Hickman, L., & Ikeda, D. (2014). *Living as learning: John Dewey in 21st Century.* Cambridge, MA: Dialogue Path Press.

Heller, P., & Rao, V. (2015). Deliberation and development. In P. Heller & V. Rao (Eds.), *Deliberation and development* (pp. 1–23). Washington, DC: World Bank Group.

Mills, C. W. (1958). *The causes of World War Three.* New York, NY: Simon and Schuster.

Mills, C. W. (1979). *Power, politics and people: The collected essays of C. Wright Mills* (2nd ed.), I. L. Horowitz (Ed.). New York: Oxford University Press.

Mills, C. W. (2000a). *The sociological imagination* (14th ed.). New York: Oxford University Press.

Mills, C. W. (2000b). *The power elite.* New York: Oxford University Press.

Mills, C. W. (2002). *White collar: The American middle class* (15th ed.). New York: Oxford University Press.

Mills, C. W. (2008). *The politics of truth: Selected writings of C. Wright Mills.* New York: Oxford University Press.

Natanson, M. (1968). Alfred Schutz on social reality and social science. *Social Research, 35*(2), 217–244.

Schutz, A. (1946). The well-informed citizen: An essay on the social distribution of knowledge. *Social Research, 13*(4) 463–478.

92 *Increased Understanding of Others*

Schutz, A. (1951). Making music together: A study in social relationship. *Social Research, 18*(1), 76–97.

Schutz, A. (1976). Equality and the meaning structure of the social world. In A. Brodersen (Ed.), *Alfred Schutz collected papers volume II* (pp. 226–273). Dordrecht, The Netherlands: Kluwer Academic Publishers.

Schutz, A. (1999). Schutz texts. In L. Embree (Ed.), *Schutzian social science* (pp. 285–318). Dordrecht, The Netherlands: Kluwer Academic Publishers.

Sigler, J. A. (1966). The political philosophy of C. Wright Mills. *Science & Society, 30*(1), 32–49.

Walsh, G. (1967). Introduction. In J. Edie & J. Wild (Eds.), *The phenomenology of the social world* (pp. xv–xxix). Evanston, Il: Northwestern University Press.

6 Individual and Community Morality

This chapter explores the possibility that individuals' and communities' morality can be developed by participating in empowered, deliberative, and expanded PB processes, which engage in deliberations about social issues. An understanding of the historical development of morality is needed because our ideas and philosophies are historically contingent and evolve over time. Gaining a better understanding of morality is important so that changes proposed for PB will promote development of individuals' and communities' morality.

The first three social philosophers examined are Ralph Waldo Emerson, Henry David Thoreau, and Walt Whitman who are all Transcendentalists. During the mid-nineteenth century, a loosely bound group of writers challenged the values of their world. They became known as Transcendentalists, and the period of their activity is sometimes referred to as the American Renaissance.

> The transcendentalists contended that ideas could be innate. By this they meant that human beings possessed ideas and understanding that came neither through the senses nor from reasoning but rather from divine inspiration – or from God's presence in the world.
>
> (Skidmore, 1998, p. 142)

Thus, they argued that people should follow their conscience. Emerson emphasized the importance of individuals' morality and the importance of self-reflection to improve it.

All Transcendentalists believed in the need for self-reflection. One of the benefits of public deliberation is that it can provoke self-reflection of one's positions concerning the issues being discussed. Because, people need to mentally prepare to defend their positions. For example, if discussions turn to how, and why, a group of people are characterized unfavorably, people will likely reflect on their own morality and possibly change their position due to new information or new arguments.

Another benefit of public deliberation is that it tends to humanize people. "The moral standards people adopt serve as guides for conduct and deterrents for detrimental activities.... Self-sanctions keep conduct in line with internal standards" (Bandura, 2012, p. 1). But, if a group of people are viewed as less than

94   *Individual and Community Morality*

human then the same moral standards would not apply. "The disengagement of moral self-sanctions from inhumane conduct is a growing human problem at both individual and collective levels" (Bandura, 1999, p. 193). The Nazis dehumanized the Jewish people, which led to the holocaust. Whenever present-day politicians refer to immigrants as animals, the immigrants are dehumanized. "There are many psychosocial maneuvers by which people selectively disengage moral self-sanctions from inhumane conduct" (Bandura, 2012, p. 1). When religion is twisted to be anti-LGBT, the LGBT community seems to be less than human. And when powerful men publically objectify women, it makes women appear to be one-dimensional and perhaps not entitled to equal pay and equal treatment.

Engaging in public deliberation with everyone can help remind us that all people are human beings.

> Voltaire put it well when he said, "Those who can make you believe absurdities can make you commit atrocities." Over the centuries, much destructive conduct has been perpetrated by ordinary, decent people in the name of righteous ideologies, religious principles, and nationalistic imperatives (Kramer, 1990; Rapoport & Alexander, 1982; Reich, 1990).
>
> (Bandura, 1999, p. 195)

In Chapter 5, Dewey's philosophy and Schutz's research support the idea that public deliberation can reduce intolerance and increase equality of opportunity. "The affirmation of common humanity can foster peaceable relationships among people (Bandura, 1999)" (Bandura, 2012, p. 4). The possible benefits would seem to make the effort more than worthwhile.

The first section is about Emerson and his efforts to provoke people to engage in self-reflection. Then, Thoreau's writings on following one's conscience lead some to conclude that he would favor local direct democracy where decisions are based on consensus. Next, it is learned that Whitman was a strong believer in democracy based on morality. John Dewey's ideas about individual and community morality and their importance to democratic governance are explored in the fourth section. Then, Mills' views of modern society's destructive effect on morality and his solution is reviewed. The final section is about the Port Huron Statement (PHS), which helped call an entire generation to action by focusing on morality.

Ralph Waldo Emerson

Emerson's primary goal was to encourage people to realize their full potential. "Emerson based his thought on the individual, not on institutions, which he considered at best to be necessary evils" (Skidmore, 1998, p. 147). He believed that individuals were the most important component of society. "I believe that Emerson was concerned more than anything with helping people gain awareness of and bring to full flower their limitless potential" (Ikeda, as cited in

Bosco et al., 2009, p. 112). The focus of his work was to help people expand their consciousness. In "Nature," Emerson wrote, "Know then, that the world exists for you. For you is the phenomenon perfect" (1983, p. 48). This encouragement of people to consider self-improvement is seen throughout his work.

Emerson saw the process of self-improvement as being an ongoing necessity. In "Self-Reliance," Emerson wrote, "A foolish consistency is the hobgoblin of little minds...With consistency a great soul has simply nothing to do" (1983, p. 265). Consistently improving one's self results in constant change within one's self.

Emerson explained in "Nature" why self-improvement was so important. "The reason why the world lacks unity and lies broken and in heaps is because man is disunited with himself" (1983, p. 47). Emerson was going to the root of the problem by advocating for and helping people improve themselves, so that they could become united with themselves. "The only basis for a social and political order that made good government possible was the morality and goodwill of the individual" (Skidmore, 1998, p. 147). As people improved themselves, their government would also be able to improve. "Governments have their origin in the moral identity of men" (Emerson, 1983, p. 566). The morality of men expresses itself in the formation of their governments.

If people failed to improve themselves, their government would suffer. "The transcendentalist believed that an unjust state depended upon the existence of a slavish people and that each person had not only the right but the duty to resist an unjust state" (Skidmore, 1998, p. 148). Thus, resistance to injustice was also part of transcendentalism.

For Emerson, an important part of self-development was morality. "The aim of Emersonian cultural criticism...is to expand powers and proliferate provocations for the moral development of human personalities" (West, 1989, p. 37). Morality was always an important part of the individual development. Emerson wrote in *His Journals*, "I have the belief that of all things the work of America is to make the advanced intelligence of mankind in the sufficiency of morals practical" (1982, p. 536). Provocation was a method used by Emerson to influence people, or as West put it, "The primary aim of Emerson's life and discourse is to provoke" (1989, p. 25). Emersonian provocation would be directed at encouraging people to think and reflect.

Emerson wanted people to reflect because he believed that only individual reflection, not authority, would be able to make people understand the truth. "Emerson, like all transcendentalists, was concerned with authority and recognized only the authority of the individual conscience that could grasp the truth through an intuition that transcended reason" (Skidmore, 1998, p. 148). Self-reflection was key to the Transcendental approach. It would enhance not only the individual, but also the community and the nation. This follows naturally the Transcendentalist view that the individual is the foundation of society. "In *Nature*, 'The American Scholar,' and the 'Divinity School Address,' Emerson called on people to break through old-fashioned formality, look within themselves once again, and return to the origins of humanity to establish a new way of life" (Ikeda, as cited in Bosco et al., 2009, p. 107).

96   *Individual and Community Morality*

A constant theme in Emerson's works is that self-reflection is a necessity for the peace and happiness of the individual, and also for the society in which he or she lives. Emerson believed that every individual has a goodness within. When man opens his mind, as Emerson said, in the "Divinity School Address," "He [man] learns that his being is without bound; that, to the good, to the perfect, he is born, low as he now lies in evil and weakness" (1983, p. 76). This shows that Emerson had a positive view of human nature.

Perhaps because of the tremendous project that Emerson set for himself, that of helping people to look within, he remained optimistic. He believed that any questions people could ask would be answerable. He wrote, "Undoubtedly we have no questions to ask which are unanswerable.... Every man's condition is a solution in hieroglyphic to those inquires he would put" (1983, p. 7). People would just need to search for and be able to decipher the answer. Every person has reason for hope because of unlimited potential.

Policy issues as a rule were not Emerson's primary concern. Nevertheless, an impulse toward helping others have hope and address injustices did lead him to address matters of policy, to a limited extent.

> He [Emerson] was drawn to politics, but only reluctantly. He spoke against the hideous treatment of Indians and against slavery ... but he was never at home in politics.... His greatest importance was as an inspiration to others who contributed more to politics directly than he did, but who might not have done so without his example.
>
> (Skidmore, 1998, p. 148)

It bears repeating that, despite his usual detachment, Emerson tried to inspire people with his writings and speeches.

Emerson's influence goes beyond those who have read his work. His work had an influence on the future development of the philosophical approach known as pragmatism. "Emerson's dominant themes of individuality, idealism, voluntarism, optimism, amelioration, and experimentation prefigure those of American pragmatism" (West, 1989, p. 35). Thus, assuredly Emerson helped to lay the groundwork for pragmatists such as John Dewey, C. Wright Mills, and others.

Henry David Thoreau

Henry David Thoreau was also a Transcendentalist. "Thoreau believed man must be allowed to cultivate the soul within him, and if allowed to do so, will bring enlightenment not just to the individual but to all" (McIntyre, 2008, p. 8). He believed that everyone could arrive at the same truth that is revealed through intuition. Thoreau believed that "we are spiritual beings, born of the same divine source and our actions must be guided by our conscious connection to that source and not by the laws of government" (McIntyre, 2008, p. 9). He believed that an individual's conscience should take precedence over any authority.

Individual and Community Morality 97

Thoreau lived at Walden Pond for over two years in order to be better able to develop and follow his conscience. He wrote, "I went to the woods because I wished to live deliberately ... and see if I could not learn what it had to teach" (Thoreau, 1968b, pp. 100–101). He wished to see how well he could live by living simply while searching for truth. Thoreau was hopeful that other people would be able to develop and follow their consciences. However, he knew that most people did not take the time to do so, and he stressed that they should find their own ways and not copy his.

For example, in *Walden*, Thoreau wrote, "The mass of men lead lives of quiet desperation" (Thoreau, 1968b, p. 8). This is because most people resigned themselves to the lives in which they found themselves. "Most men, even in this comparatively free country, through mere ignorance and mistake, are so occupied with the factitious cares and superfluously coarse labors of life that its finer fruits cannot be plucked by them" (Thoreau, 1968b, p. 6). People get so caught up in their day-to-day lives that they lose sight of what is most important, and thus make it impossible to find full development.

In another example, in *Walden*, Thoreau explains how easy it is for people to fall into destructive physical and mental habits.

It is remarkable how easily and insensibly we fall into a particular route, and make a beaten track for ourselves.... The surface of the earth is soft and impressible by the feet of men; and so with the paths which the mind travels.

(Thoreau, 1968b, pp. 355–356)

People are susceptible to forming habits in the daily routes we take as well as forming habits in the way we think about things.

On the other hand, Thoreau was optimistic about the ability of people to improve their lives. He wrote, "I know of no more encouraging fact than the unquestionable ability of man to elevate his life by a conscious endeavor" (1968b, p. 100). He suggests a path people could take to elevate their lives when he defines the value of a true friend. "A friend is one who incessantly pays us the compliment of expecting from us all the virtues in us. It takes two to speak the truth – one to speak, and another to hear" (Thoreau, 1986a, p. 283). Thoreau seems to recognize that this type of friendship is not commonplace when he writes, "In our daily intercourse with men, our nobler faculties are dormant and suffered to rust" (1986a, p. 284). Thus, a true friend would help to drive people to keep improving their lives.

In addition to friends, Thoreau also recognized the need for good neighbors. In *Walden*, in his discussion about building his cabin, he wrote, "At length, in the beginning of May, with the help of some of my acquaintances, rather to improve so good an occasion for neighborliness than from any necessity, I set up the frame of my house" (1986b, p. 49). Thoreau believed that neighborliness should be an important goal regardless of whether the neighbors are actually needed to be included in a particular project. Also, in "Resistance to Civil Government," Thoreau wrote, "I have never declined paying the highway tax, because I am as desirous of being a good neighbor as I am of being a bad

98   *Individual and Community Morality*

subject" (Thoreau, 1996, p. 17). He was more concerned with being a good neighbor than with being a good citizen, as defined by the government.

Thoreau advocated breaking any laws passed by the government which required an individual to violate his conscience. In "Resistance to Civil Government," he wrote, "How can a man be satisfied to entertain an opinion merely and enjoy it" (Thoreau, 1996, p. 8)? People have a responsibility to themselves to act in harmony with their conscience.

> Action from principle, – the perception and the performance of right, – changes things and relations; it is essentially revolutionary, and does not consist wholly with any thing which was. It not only divides states and churches, it divides families; aye, it divides the individual, separating the diabolical in him from the divine.
>
> (Thoreau, 1996, p. 8)

In order to better themselves, in matters of importance people need to act on their principles, regardless of the consequences.

Of course, many people fear the consequences of disobeying the State, for themselves and their families. A consequence of Thoreau's not paying the poll-tax, in order to protest slavery, was jail. After one night there, he was released when someone "interfered" and paid his past due taxes (Thoreau, 1996). Thoreau wrote,

> if I deny the authority of the State when it presents its tax-bill, it will soon take and waste all my property, and so harass me and my children without end.... It costs me less in some sense to incur the penalty of disobedience to the State, than it would to obey.
>
> (Thoreau, 1996, pp. 12–13)

Thoreau felt it was more important to be true to one's own self and protest an unjust law than to obey an unjust law.

Of course, in Thoreau's time, slavery was the most egregious practice supported by the government. In "Resistance to Civil Government," Thoreau wrote,

> if it is of such a nature that it requires you to be the agent of injustice to another, then, I say, break the law. Let your life be a counter friction to stop the machine. What I have to do is to see, at any rate, that I do not lend myself to the wrong which I condemn.
>
> (Thoreau, 1996, p. 9)

For Thoreau, this was a line which he would not cross regardless of the consequences. And in 1850, the Fugitive Slave Law required people in northern anti-slave states to cooperate in returning escaped slaves to their masters, which made everyone who obeyed the law agents of injustice.

This led Thoreau to write in "Slavery in Massachusetts" that, "The majority of the men of the North, and of the South, and East, and West, are not men of

Individual and Community Morality 99

principle" (Thoreau, 1996, p. 131). People of principle would not support the national or state governments because they all actively supported slavery. As a rule, Thoreau opposed violence. He did admire John Brown, however. Brown was hanged for treason after he and his supporters raided an arsenal at Harper's Ferry, Virginia, in an attempt to inspire a slave revolt. In "A Plea for Captain John Brown," Thoreau wrote, "He was a superior man. He did not value his bodily life in comparison with ideal things" (Thoreau, 1996, p. 147). Some ideals are worth risking your life, by directly opposing the government.

Walt Whitman

Walt Whitman was a Transcendentalist writer who expressed his convictions, thoughts, and emotions in both poetry and prose. Whitman's major themes were equality and democracy. His goal seems to have been equality for all human beings in all aspects of life.

One way that Whitman advocated equality was by saying that we are all the same. In "Song of Myself" he wrote, "In all people I see myself, none more and not one a barleycorn less. /And the good or bad I say of myself I say of them" (1982, p. 45). Whitman believed that none of us are any better or worse than anyone else, because he can see himself in everyone else. By writing about himself, Whitman was writing about everyone. In "Song of Myself," he wrote, "I celebrate myself, /And what I assume you shall assume, /For every atom belonging to me as good belongs to you" (Whitman, 1982, p. 27). In celebrating himself, he is celebrating everyone. Kateb offered a possible definition for atom in the verse when he wrote, "An atom is a potentiality, I think" (2014, p. 23). Thus, in "Song of Myself," Whitman says that we all have the same potentials and it is only our cultural settings that determine who we are and what we become (Kateb, 2014). In other words, we could look at anyone and say there but for the grace of God, go I.

Given Whitman's conviction that we are all the same, it is understandable that he would stand up for the rights of others. In "Song of Myself," he wrote, "I will not have a single person slighted or left away..." (1982, p. 44). Whitman left no doubt that he considered slaves to be like any other person, when he wrote, "I am the hounded slave .... I wince at the bite of the dogs (1982, p. 65). He felt the pain of others, including slaves and convicts in prison. In "Song of Myself," he wrote, "I become any presence or truth of humanity here, /And see myself in prison shaped like another man,/And feel the dull unintermitted pain" (Whitman, 1982, p. 70). Prisons shape people and make them different. But, were we there, we would be shaped in the same manner.

Whitman was also a defender of women's rights. In "Song of Myself," he wrote,

> I am the poet of the woman the same as the man,
> And I say it is as great to be a woman as to be a man,
> And I say there is nothing greater than the mother of men.

(1982, p. 46)

100   *Individual and Community Morality*

Whitman saw the goodness in all people, regardless of sex, and was able to identify with all people.

Whitman also foreshadowed the homosexual rights movement. In the Calamus series of poems in *Leaves of Grass*, he wrote about homosexual love. "Whitman insistently pursues these themes [sexual and bodily themes] throughout his career, holding that the appropriate conception of democratic love cannot be articulated without forging a new attitude toward both the body and its sexuality" (Nussbaum, 2014, p. 97). Whitman broke away from the Puritan tradition of hiding sexuality and not talking about it. In "I Sing the Body Electric" Whitman wrote, "If life and the soul are sacred the human body is sacred" (1982, p. 124). Since the body is sacred, there is no reason to be ashamed of any part of it. In "By Blue Ontario's Shore," Whitman wrote, "Underneath all is the Expression of love for men and women" (1982, p. 481). Whitman felt that love is fundamental to human life. Thus, it needs to be considered – even to be written about.

Another major theme in Whitman's work was democracy. Whitman understood that for a democratic government to function best, there needed to be a reconciliation between the individual and society. In "Democratic Vistas," he wrote,

> But the mass, or lump character, for imperative reasons, is to be ever carefully weigh'd, borne in mind, and provided for. Only from its proper regulation and potency, comes the other, comes the chance of individualism. The two are contradictory, but our task is to reconcile them.
>
> (1982, pp. 940–941)

Only a supportive society will encourage the development of individualism. Whitman further commented on the reconciliation of individualism and mass society when he wrote,

> I have no doubt myself that the two will merge, and will mutually profit and brace each other, and that from them a greater product, a third, will arise. But I feel that at present they and their oppositions form a serious problem and paradox in the United States.
>
> (1982, p. 941)

Whitman anticipated that this reconciliation would benefit both the individual and society as well as producing additional benefits.[1]

Whitman's treatment of death seems to be a way to encourage reconciliation. He helps us accept death by saying that life never really ends. In "Song of Myself," he writes, "And I know I am deathless" (1982, p. 46). He writes that people are reborn after they die. "And as to you life; I reckon you are the leavings of many deaths, /No doubt I have died myself ten thousand times before" (1982, p. 86). Whitman helps us to accept death as not being final. This leads "to an acceptance of mortality, finitude, and loss, to enable us to mourn and

Individual and Community Morality   101

therefore adequately to love" (Nussbaum, 2014, p. 122). Because everyone "capable of mourning, can let go of hate, and disgust, and pursue a truly inclusive love" (Nussbaum, 2014, p. 124). Death can be a new beginning not only for the dying, but also for those left behind. This can be seen in the poems Whitman wrote to honor the memory of President Lincoln. In "When Lilacs Last in the Door Yard Bloom'd," he wrote,

> O what shall I hang on the chamber walls?
> And what shall the pictures be that I hang on the walls,
> To adorn the burial-house of him I love?
> Pictures of growing spring and farms and homes ...
> And all the scenes of life and the workshops, and the
> workmen homeward returning.
>
> (Whitman, 1982, p. 462)

He felt that the best memorial to President Lincoln would be pictures representing life, harmony, and love. Whitman believed that love undergirded everything.

Another way Whitman encouraged reconciliation among people was to stress that there are limits to our knowledge, and that the unknown is not to be feared. In "Song of Myself," he wrote,

> And I call to mankind, Be not curious about God,
> For I who am curious about each am not curious about God,
> No array of terms can say how much I am at peace about God and death.
>
> (1982, p. 85)

For Whitman, the unknowable should be accepted. In "A Song of the Rolling Earth," he wrote, "I swear I see what is better than to tell the best, /It is always to leave the best untold.... The best of the earth cannot be told anyhow" (1982, p. 367). Whitman did not attempt to explain the unknown.

Whitman did not try to explain the unknown because he knew that faith could interpret it. In "Democratic Vistas," he wrote, "Faith, very old, now scared away by science, must be restored, brought back by the same power that caused her departure – restored with new sway, deeper, wider, higher than ever" (1982, p. 988). Whitman felt that faith was important because it tends to complement realism. In "Democratic Vistas," he wrote, "let us take our stand, our ground, and never desert it, to confront the growing excess of arrogance of realism" (1982, p. 983). Whitman believed that there is a moral purpose in life that realism is insufficient to explain. In "Democratic Vistas," he wrote,

> The librarian of Congress in a paper read before the Social Science Convention at New York, October, 1869, [said] "The true question to ask respecting a book, is, *has it help'd any human soul?*" This is the hint, statement, not only of the great literatus, his book, but of every great artist.
>
> (1982, p. 987)

102 *Individual and Community Morality*

The moral purpose of life is to help another human soul. In particular, Whitman believed that any artistic work should be judged by this standard.

Whitman believed that every individual had a moral sense within, and that it was the duty of great literature to help people discover and develop this moral sense. In "Democratic Vistas," he wrote,

> That which really balances and conserves the social and political world is not so much legislation, police, treaties, and dread of punishment, as the latent eternal intuitional sense, in humanity, of fairness, manliness, decorum, &c. Indeed, this perennial regulation, control, and oversite, by self-suppliance, is *sine qua non* to democracy; and a highest widest aim of democratic literature may well be to bring forth, cultivate, brace, and strengthen this sense in individuals and society.
>
> (1982, p. 989)

Whitman believed that both individuals and society had a moral sense which democratic literature needed to reveal and support.

Walt Whitman was a strong supporter of democracy. In "Democratic Vistas," he wrote:

> The purpose of democracy – supplanting old beliefs in the necessary absoluteness of establish'd dynastic rulership, temporal, ecclesiastical, and scholastic, as furnishing the only security against chaos, crime, and ignorance.... *This*, as matters now stand in our civilized world, is the only scheme worth working from, as warranting results like those of Nature's laws, reliable, when once establish'd, to carry on themselves.
>
> (1982, p. 942)

The reason for democracy is to replace rule by elite families, rule by the educated, the church, or secular authority. Also, Whitman maintains that democracy provides the only real security for the people, because the people make the decisions.

In addition to security, Whitman asserts, again in "Democratic Vistas," that democracy tends to bind people together. "And, topping democracy, this most alluring record, that it alone can bind, all nations, all men, of however various and distant lands, into a brotherhood, a family" (Whitman, 1982, pp. 948–949). This would, of course, give the individual a sense of belonging,[2] as well as allowing the masses to work more smoothly together.

Another benefit of democracy is that it is a cure for generalized discontent. Again, in "Democratic Vistas," Whitman said:

> the theory of a wider democratizing of intuitions in any civilized country, much trouble might well be saved to all European lands by recognizing this palpable fact, (for a palpable fact it is), that some form of such democratizing is about the only resource now left. *That*, or chronic dissatisfaction

Individual and Community Morality   103

continued, mutterings which grow annually louder and louder, till, in due course, and pretty swiftly in most cases, the inevitable crisis, crash, dynastic ruin.

(1982, p. 950)

The choice is between democratizing intuitions or chronic dissatisfaction of the people which may lead to eventual crisis.

In conclusion, Whitman advocated for equality for everyone including women, slaves, and sexual minorities. Of course, equality is a core democratic norm. Whitman also supported democracy because it tended to give people a sense of belonging. He saw the reconciliation of individualism and mass society as critically necessary as well as a paradox. Perhaps individuals could improve their capabilities if they became the local government, as proposed in this study. Whitman believed that the moral purpose of life is to help another human soul. A community of empowered individuals would certainly have the capacity to help other people.

John Dewey

This section examines how Dewey's political philosophy relates to morality. Specifically, Dewey's philosophy of democracy is reviewed, including his ideal of democracy and the morality upon which it would be based. And finally, it is proposed that a properly designed PB process could be the political vehicle to get us from here, our current situation, to there, Dewey's democratic ideal.

Discussion and deliberation within the community can not only help develop an individual's capacities, it can also help bring the individual's interests and community's interests into alignment, including ethical standards.

Democracy, in a word, is social, that is to say, an ethical conception, and upon its significance is based its significance as governmental. Democracy is a form of government only because it is a form of moral and spiritual association.

(Dewey, 1993b, p. 59)

Having a shared perception of right and wrong helps to give direction to a democratic government.

Morals are lessons we learn as children; and they are concepts we refine as we grow older. "Morals are social" (Dewey, 2002, p. 319). It makes sense that the more we engage in discussion and deliberation within our community, the more our morals are fine-tuned and converge. What is important are the actions we take as a result of our morals. "Morality resides not in perception of fact, but in the use made of its perception" (Dewey, 2002, p. 298). This is a reflection of the character of people. "Dewey offers not a program, but rather a political morality – an ethic of self-government and self-realization through collective life" (Morris & Shapiro, 1993, p. xii). People are able to improve themselves by

104 *Individual and Community Morality*

working with others on community problems. Democracy provides people the opportunity to express their morality.

Democracy allows for the expression of the character of the people. "The democratic faith in human equality is belief that every human being, independent of the quantity or range of his personal endowment, has the right to equal opportunity with every other person for development of whatever gifts he has" (Dewey, 1993a, p. 242). Society's belief in human equality is an example of individual's character defining the community's character.

> It [equality] denotes effective regard for whatever is distinctive and unique in each, irrespective of physical and psychological inequalities. It [equality] is not a natural possession but is a fruit of the community when its action is directed by its character as a community.
>
> (Dewey, 1954, p. 151)

The character of the community is revealed through relationships among community members.

Dewey believed that democracy could be, and should be, a way of life. "Democracy is a way of personal life controlled not merely by faith in human nature in general but by faith in the capacity of human beings for intelligent judgement and action if proper conditions are furnished" (Dewey, 1993a, p. 242). Dewey promoted the idea of democracy as being a way of life because he knew that for our democracy to work as it was intended, people needed to become actively involved. In "Creative Democracy – The Task Before Us," Dewey wrote,

> If what has been said is charged with being a set of moral commonplaces, my only reply is that is just the point in saying them. For to get rid of the habit of thinking of democracy as something institutional and external and to acquire the habit of treating it as a way of personal life is to realize that democracy is a moral ideal and so far as it becomes a fact is a moral fact. It is to realize that democracy is a reality only as it is indeed a commonplace of living.
>
> (1993a, p. 244)

Democracy can become more than the democratic institutions which were established in our constitution.

The quality of local governance is improved when the morals of the community are debated, which results in the public morals being refined and shaped to more closely match the morals of the individuals in the community. Thus, the political morality, as practiced by government, more closely reflects the will of the people. Of course, public morality is reflected in who is elected as well as which policies are enacted. "That government exists to serve its community, and that this purpose cannot be achieved unless the community itself shares in selecting its governors and determining their policies" (Dewey, 1954, p. 146). Thus,

Individual and Community Morality   105

individuals must take responsibility, not only for helping to define political morality and electing politicians, but also for the policies which are meant to reflect the community morals.

Dewey was able to envision that a democratic society would contain local publics where all voices could be heard. However, Dewey did not propose exactly how we could get to that point. "The long-term democratization of American life awaits a political technology and vehicle not yet fully in view" (Tillman, 1987, p. 1396). I propose that an empowered, deliberative, and expanded PB process could be just such a political vehicle. Thus, we may yet be able to make Dewey's vision a reality.

C. Wright Mills

Mills believed that in modern society our values, for both individuals and society, were in decline, due to several causes.

> There are many reasons for this banalization of old values and the failure to create new and viable ones. There is the recent growth of big cities, where men live without local roots and relations are impersonal, individualist and blasé. There is the residential and business movement from state to state and city to city which further weakens the close, informal controls of personal relations and deeply-felt communities of interest. There is the shrinkage in family life ... This is, in short, the great unsettling of many people without personal ties, family continuity, or community relations.
>
> (Mills, 1979, p. 333)

There are many troubling consequences to the loss of values among individuals and communities, including an increasing priority to make money. "The pursuit of the moneyed life is the commanding value, in relation to which the influence of other values has declined, so men easily become morally ruthless in the pursuit of easy money and fast estate-building" (Mills, 1979, p. 334). This can lead to a generalized immorality throughout society.

The lack of a moral foundation can result in a moral insensibility. Mills, in *The Causes of World War Three*, gave the following definition of moral insensibility: "By moral insensibility, in short, I mean the incapacity for moral reaction to event and to character, to high decision and to the drift of human circumstance" (1958, p. 77). In other words, we lose our sense of moral outrage and our ability for moral judgment.

Mass media have the effect of being a distraction in modern life, which is compounded by the issue of moral insensitivity in modern life. "But regardless of the reasons, the absence of any moral order of belief exposes us to the influences of a commercial culture, the mass media manipulations of frenzied entertainment and distraction" (Mills, 1979, pp. 333–334). We are ready to accept alternative moral codes presented in popular culture.

106   *Individual and Community Morality*

Commercial jazz, soap opera, pulp fiction, comic strips, the movies set the images, mannerisms, standards, and aims of the urban masses. In one way or another, everyone is equal before these cultural machines; like technology itself, the mass media are nearly universal in their incidence and appeal. They are a kind of common denominator, a kind of scheme for pre-scheduled, mass emotions.

(Mills, 2002, p. 333)

The mass media define our heroes, which we try to emulate, and the cultural myths, which we accept. "The truth is as the media are now organized, they expropriate our vision" (Mills, 2002, p. 333). Thus, the mass media contributes to our moral confusion and misdirection.

Mills' solution, as reported in the previous chapter, was for people to actively engage in small publics discussing the issues of most importance. An empowered PB process with expanded funding and responsibilities that engages in public deliberation would meet Mills' requirements. People could regain a moral direction.

Port Huron Statement

Tom Hayden wrote the original draft of the Port Huron Statement for the Students for a Democratic Society (SDS). The result is generally considered to be the manifesto of the New Left. "[T]he Statement represents the collective thought of the inspirational founding Convention of SDS, held in Port Huron, Michigan, June, 11–15, 1962" (Hayden, 2005, p. 43). The conference attendees rewrote the original draft and published it as SDS's founding document to express their beliefs about social change. The statement's central theme is using participatory democracy to overcome apathy and effect social change. "Despite the eclectic and even diffuse character of the Port Huron Statement, it expressed a central idea embodied in the phrase "participatory democracy" (Flacks, 2015, p. 225). As Hayden later wrote, "We were rebelling against the experience of apathy not against a single specific oppression" (2005, p. 4). The SDS wanted to connect all of the issues of their time.

These students could see the possibilities of addressing all the issues of the day if the people could be awakened from their apathy and engage the moral issues. "Their [SDS's] immediate hope was to enable students engaged in the civil rights struggle to see a common political agenda with those concerned with ending the Cold War" (Flacks, 2015, p. 225). These two political fights are connected with several social justice issues. In the Port Huron Statement, they wrote,

The fight for civil rights is also one for social welfare for all Americans; for free speech and the right to protest; for the shield of economic independence and bargaining power; for the reduction of the arms race which takes national attention and resources away from the problems of domestic injustices.

(Hayden, 2005, p. 162)

Individual and Community Morality   107

The SDS saw participatory democracy as empowering people to make moral choices. Because the Port Huron Statement focused on people making moral choices, the "values" section is first, after the introduction. Hayden wrote,

> We chose to put "values" forward as the first priority in challenging the conditions of apathy and forging a new politics. Embracing values meant making choices as morally autonomous human beings against a world that advertised in every possible way that there were no choices.
>
> (2005, p. 5)

One of the values put forward in the Port Huron Statement is that people have unfulfilled potential. In the "values" section, they wrote, "We regard men as infinitely precious and possessed of unfulfilled capacities for reason, freedom, and love" (Hayden, 2005, p. 51). A little further on, they wrote, "Men have unrealized potential for self-cultivation, self-direction, self-understanding, and creativity" (Hayden, 2005, p. 52). Of course, people who have these capacities would be able participate in democratic governance as well as participating in a broader democratic society.

The Port Huron Statement agreed with both Dewey and Mills in asserting that both the individual and the community would benefit from participatory democracy. In 2015, Hayden wrote,

> It [participatory democracy] was a way of empowering the individual as autonomous but interdependent with other individuals, and the community as a civic society. Without this empowerment on both levels, the Statement warned, we were living in "a democracy without publics," in the phrase of C. Wright Mills, the rebel sociologist who was one of our intellectual heroes.
>
> (2015, p. 21)

In addition to Dewey and Mills, the North American tribal governance, Thomas Jefferson, and Henry David Thoreau were part of the legacy that the Port Huron Statement was built upon (Hayden, 2005). Hayden, in 2005, wrote,

> Perhaps the most compelling advocate of participatory democracy, however, was Henry David Thoreau, the nineteenth-century author of *Civil Disobedience*, who opposed taxation for either slavery or war.... Thoreau's words were often repeated in the early days of the sixties civil rights and antiwar movements.
>
> (2005, p. 6)

There is a long tradition in the United States supporting participatory democracy.

Concerning Dewey, Richard Flacks, one of the participants in the conference about the Port Huron Statement wrote,

108   *Individual and Community Morality*

> [I]nsofar as the U.S. New Left stressed the need to learn from and respond to lived experience, to be experimental and non-dogmatic about issues of strategy, to be open and heterodox ideologically, to emphasize the educative character of social action, to refuse any large-scale theory of history, to question authority, to maintain organizational fluidity, to emphasize face-to-face decision making, to stress personal growth as a measure of political validity, it was John Dewey's project that was being implemented.
>
> (2015, pp. 237–238)

Dewey's writings influenced the writing of the Port Huron Statement. "Perhaps nowhere did Dewey's ideals echo more resoundingly than in the 'Port Huron Statement' (1962)" (Westbrook, 1991, p. 549). An important goal for Dewey was a truly deliberative society.

In addition to examining the philosophical foundations of the Port Huron Statement, it is useful to look at events immediately preceding and coinciding with writing the Port Huron Statement. "It is generally accepted that the New Left arose out of mobilization on behalf of Civil Rights" (Tarrow, 2016, p. 812). The Student Nonviolent Coordinating Committee (SNCC) was an inspiration to many young people, including the some of the founders of the SDS, who wrote the Port Huron Statement.

> SNCC grew out of a lunch counter sit-in by four African American students in Greensboro, South Carolina. Hayden and Paul Potter, another SDS founder, went to Mississippi to help organize along with SNCC activists and were badly beaten and jailed by local whites.
>
> (Xenos, 2016, p. 814)

People involved in the struggle for civil rights were willing to risk their lives for the sake of social justice.

Everyone involved in the civil rights movement struggle knew the importance of human dignity. Hayden wrote, "For virtually every early member of SDS, the rural, southern African American movement as exemplified in SNCC was both political model and moral exemplar" (2005, p. 6). The SNCC's use of direct action, such as the lunch counter sit-in, was an important method that was used by the SDS. In 2005, Hayden wrote, "participation in direct action was a method of psychic empowerment, a fulfillment of human potential, a means of curing alienation, as well as an effective means of mass protest" (2005, p. 7). Both the SNCC and the SDS knew the importance of direct action, as a way of learning by doing.

The other important method used by the SNCC was consciousness-raising, which involved raising individuals' awareness of their right to make decisions (Hayden, 2005). Consciousness-raising is done in small group discussions. In writing about how activists from that time period did their work, Hayden wrote,

> The idea was to challenge elite authority by direct example on the one hand, and on the other to draw "ordinary people," whether apathetic students,

Individual and Community Morality   109

sharecroppers, or office workers, into a dawning belief in their right to participate in decisions. This was the method – call it consciousness-raising – of the Student Nonviolent Coordinating Committee, which influenced SDS, the early women's liberation groups, farm workers' house meetings, and Catholic base communities, eventually spreading to Vietnam veterans' rap groups and other organizations. Participatory democracy was a tactic of movement building as well as an end in itself. And by an insistence on listening to "the people" as a basic ethic of participatory democracy, the early movement was able to guarantee its roots in American culture and traditions while avoiding the imported ideologies that infected many elements of the earlier left.

(2005, pp. 8–9)

Consciousness-raising describes individuals becoming aware of their own value and rights, by people listening to them and giving them a sense of empowerment. The values promoted by the Port Huron Statement and the SDS is why they were successful in promoting the civil rights movement, as well as being a foundation for movements started later in the 1960s, such as the women's liberation movement. "The Port Huron preoccupations reflected the issues of the already emerging 1960s movements, and the manifesto then lent energy to the movements" (Piven, 2016, p. 809). As Hayden wrote in 2005, "The Port Huron Statement called for a coalescing of social movements: civil rights, peace, labor, liberals, and students" (p. 14).

The Port Huron Statement helped lay the groundwork for the women's liberation movement even though the Statement used only male pronouns and no mention was made of women's rights. Ackelsberg and Shanley wrote,

Our own teaching and writing on gender justice, then, stemmed both from our having shared the conviction of the PHS [Port Huron Statement] authors that social change in the direction of greater justice and equality was possible, and from our increasing awareness that gender justice would have to be an essential aspect of any vision of social justice worth fighting for.

(2016, p. 799)

The Port Huron Statement connected with the women's liberation movement concerning the values and direction of society, as a whole.

Consciousness-raising is something else that the women's liberation movement has in common with the SDS and the Port Huron Statement.

[T]he women's movement grew out of the experiences of consciousness-raising, and argued that "the personal is political." Members of consciousness-raising groups drew on their personal experiences in order to uncover shared experiences that – they/we came to recognize – arose from social norms and social structures.... Consciousness raising was an extremely important analytic tool, a valuable methodology for the shaping of feminist analysis and theory.

(Ackelsberg & Shanley, 2016, p. 800)

110 *Individual and Community Morality*

Consciousness-raising was a key part of the social movements reviewed in this study and a prerequisite for direct action.

The methodology of participatory democracy, in general, and consciousness-raising, in particular, were addressed toward the end of the "values" section. The Port Huron Statement examines how participatory democracy works by looking at its fundamental elements.

> In a participatory democracy, the political life would be based on several root principles.
>
> [1] that decision-making of basic social consequence be carried on by public groupings;
> [2] that politics be seen positively, as the art of collectively creating an acceptable pattern of social relations;
> [3] that politics has the function of bring people out of isolation and into community, thus being a necessary, though not sufficient, means of finding meaning in personal life; that the political order should serve to clarify problems in a way instrumental to their solution; it should provide outlets for the expression of personal grievance and aspiration; opposing views should be organized so as to illuminate choices and facilitate the attainment of goals; channels should be commonly available, to relate men to knowledge and to power so that private problems – from bad recreational facilities to personal alienation – are formulated as general issues.
>
> (Hayden, 2005, pp. 53–54)

The part of the third point – about how important it is for people to be able to translate private problems into general issues – has been described, in part, as consciousness-raising. A well-designed PB process, within the legal restrictions on the scope of issues, addresses the other principles of participatory democracy.

In addition to strongly supporting the Civil Rights movement and helping to inspire the women's liberation movement, the Port Huron Statement also helped other social movements.

> The Civil Rights movement also helped to give birth to a sister movement of the minority poor in the northern cities that succeeded in forcing expansion of U.S. social welfare programs. And as the war in Southeast Asia escalated, the Port Huron thinkers became the intellectual leaders of the antiwar movement, whose repercussions eventually forced the American war machine to withdraw. So, Port Huron was important, and it was the movements to which the statement lent purpose, coherence, and élan that made it important.
>
> (Piven, 2016, p. 809)

Social movements have been an important force in advocating for progressive issues. The Port Huron Statement is able to support such seemingly diverse

Individual and Community Morality 111

social movements because it focused on basic values, such as human dignity, and the direct participation of the people.

The legacy of the Port Huron Statement includes its support for the civil rights movement and its advocacy for participatory democracy, to overcome apathy and effect social change. The authors of the Port Huron Statement believed in the unlimited potential of people and their ability to make moral choices.

Mills, as noted in the previous chapter, wanted social scientists to give themselves the task of translating "personal troubles into public issues" (Mills, 2000, p. 187), in order to provide publics with relevant issues that they could deliberate and decide. In the 1960s, this task was accomplished with consciousness-raising groups. The importance of translating personal troubles into general issues was noted in the Port Huron Statement, as a root principle upon which participatory democracy is based. The Port Huron Statement provided a passion that helped fuel the social movements of the 1960s.

An empowered PB process that engages in public deliberation about community issues revolving around the morality of how people are treated could have a similar effect on today's society. Public deliberation about issues concerning morality could encourage people to reflect and reconsider the basis of their beliefs. For example, discussions about homelessness might cause some to reflect on what would be the morally right thing to do. The proposed open discussions might be a good place to start such discussions. It would not be easy to confront such issues. But it may be harder, in the long run, not to.

Notes

1 Perhaps Jefferson's ward system proposal, as explained in Chapter 4, would have been a means to this reconciliation. In which case, public happiness would be the additional benefit produced from such a reconciliation.
2 In Chapter 7, it was noted that one way the League of the Iroquois was able to maintain its system of governance was by instilling a strong sense of belonging.

References

Ackelsberg, M., & Shanley, M. (2016). The Port Huron statement and political science. *American Political Science Association, 14*(3), 799–800. doi: 1017/S15375927116001213

Bandura, A. (2012). Moral disengagement. In D. Christie (Ed.), *The encyclopedia of peace psychology* (pp. 1–5). Blackwell Publishing Ltd. Retrieved from https://online library.wiley.com/doi/pdf/10.1002/9780470672532.wbepp. 165

Bandura, A. (1999). Moral disengagement in the perpetration of inhumanities. *Personality and Social Psychology Review, 3*(3), 193–209.

Bosco, R., Myerson, J., & Ikeda, D. (2009). *Creating Waldens: An east-west conversation on the American renaissance.* Cambridge, MA: Dialogue Path Press.

Dewey, J. (1954). *The public and its problems.* Athens, OH: Swallow Press/Ohio University Press Books.

Dewey, J. (1993a). Creative democracy: The task before us. In D. Morris & I. Shapiro (Eds.), *John Dewey: The political writings* (pp. 240–245). Indianapolis, IN: Hackett Publishing Company.

112 *Individual and Community Morality*

Dewey, J. (1993b). The ethics of democracy. In D. Morris & I. Shapiro (Eds.), *John Dewey: The political writings* (pp. 59–65). Indianapolis, IN: Hackett Publishing Company.

Dewey, J. (2002). *Human nature and conduct* (2nd ed.). Toronto, Canada: General Publishing Company.

Emerson, R. (1982). *Emerson in his journals*. Cambridge, MA: Harvard University Press.

Emerson, R. (1983). *Ralph Waldo Emerson: Essays and lectures* (4th ed.). New York: The Library of America.

Flacks, R. (2015). Philosophical and political roots of the American new left. In R. Flacks & N. Lichtenstein (Eds.), *The Port Huron statement: Sources and legacies of the new left's founding manifesto* (pp. 224–238). Philadelphia, PA: University of Pennsylvania Press.

Hayden, T. (2005). *The Port Huron statement: The visionary call of the 1960s revolution.* New York: Thunder's Mouth Press.

Hayden, T. (2015). Crafting the Port Huron statement: Measuring its impact in the 1960s and after. In R. Flacks & N. Lichtenstein (Eds.), *The Port Huron statement: Sources and legacies of the new left's founding manifesto* (pp. 16–35). Philadelphia, PA: University of Pennsylvania Press.

Kateb, G. (2014). Walt Whitman and the culture of democracy. In J. E. Seery (Ed.), *A political companion to Walt Whitman* (2nd ed.) (pp. 19–45). Lexington, KY: The University Press of Kentucky.

McIntyre, C. (2008). The politics of Thoreau: A spiritual intent. *The Thoreau Society Bulletin*, (262), 7–9. Retrieved from www.jstor.org/stable/23402794

Mills, C. W. (1958). *The causes of World War Three*. New York: Simon and Schuster.

Mills, C. W. (1979). *Power, politics and people: The collected essays of C. Wright Mills* (2nd ed.), I. L. Horowitz (Ed.). New York: Oxford University Press.

Mills, C. W. (2000). *The sociological imagination* (14th ed.). New York: Oxford University Press.

Mills, C. W. (2002). *White collar: The American middle class* (15th ed.). New York: Oxford University Press.

Morris, D., & Shapiro, I. (1993) Editor's introduction. In D. Morris & I. Shapiro (Eds.), *John Dewey: The political writings* (pp. ix–xix). Indianapolis, IN: Hackett Publishing Company.

Nussbaum, M. C. (2014). Democratic desire: Walt Whitman. In J. E. Seery (Ed.). *A political companion to Walt Whitman* (2nd ed.) (pp. 96–126). Lexington, KY: The University Press of Kentucky.

Piven, F. (2016). The Port Huron statement and political science. *American Political Science Association, 14*(3), 809. doi: 10.1017/S1537592716001250

Skidmore, M. J. (1998). *Legacy to the world: A study of America's political ideas.* New York: Peter Lang Publishing.

Tarrow, S. (2016). The Port Huron statement and political science. *American Political Science Association, 14*(3), 812–813. doi: 10.1017/S1537592716001274

Thoreau, H. D. (1968a). *The writings of Henry David Thoreau* (Vol. 1, 2nd ed.). New York: AMS Press.

Thoreau, H. D. (1968b). *The writings of Henry David Thoreau* (Vol. 2, 2nd ed.). New York: AMS Press.

Thoreau, H. D. (1996). *Thoreau political writings*, N. L. Rosenblum (Ed.). Cambridge: Cambridge University Press.

Tilman, R. (1987). The neoinstrumental theory of democracy. *Journal of Economic Issues, 21*(3), 1379–1401.

West, C. (1989). *The American evasion of philosophy: A genealogy of pragmatism.* London: Macmillan Press.

Westbrook, R. B. (1991). *John Dewey and American democracy.* Ithaca, NY: Cornell University Press.

Whitman, W. (1982). *Whitman: Poetry and prose.* New York: The Library of America.

Xenos, N. (2016). The Port Huron statement and political science. *American Political Science Association, 14*(3), 814–815. doi: 10.1017/S1537592716001286

7 A Sense of Belonging

Another potential benefit of PB is that it could help create a sense of belonging within communities. All the potential benefits are intertwined and tend to reinforce one another. People with a strong sense of belonging could result in people volunteering to do as much as possible for their community. This could result in feelings of public happiness, increased understanding of others, and possibly a more developed morality if the resulting community discussions included issues about the ethics of behavior. Conversely, the other potential benefits would tend to create and reinforce a sense of belonging.

This chapter begins by looking at the Iroquois Indians. Their successful democracy could be attributed, in part, to their strong sense of belonging. This example shows that it is possible for an entire society to have a strong sense of belonging.

The second section contains Mills' analysis of society's current lack of a sense of belonging and his conclusion that it is really a lack of a political sense of belonging. Next, how and why participants in PB can develop a sense of belonging is examined by reviewing Talpin's theory of self-change. The last section is about Robert Putnam's social capital and how it relates to a sense of belonging. This section begins with a brief examination of the history of the social capital concept. Then, the capital debate controversy of social capital is addressed. The last subsection reviews Putnam's understanding of social capital and why Putnam's idea of social capital works in the PB process.

The League of the Iroquois

There was an established democracy in North America long before the first colonialists landed in New England. The League of the Iroquois, or Haudenosaunee, also known as the Five Tribes (Senecas, Onondagas, Oneidas, Mohawks, and Cayugas), until the Tuscaroras tribe became the sixth tribe to join the confederation, had a functioning democratic government for perhaps hundreds of years before the Mayflower set anchor at Plymouth Rock in 1620.

A wide range of estimates exist for the founding date of the confederacy. Iroquoian sources, using oral history and recollections of family ancestries (the traditional methods for marking time through history), have fixed the

origin date at between 1000 and 1400 A.D.; Euro-American historians have tended to place the origin of the Iroquois league at about 1450.
(Johansen, 1982, pp. 21–22)

Whatever the date of the founding, the purpose was to put an end to war between the tribes by agreeing to an oral constitution, known as the Great Law of Peace. Around 1880, the Great Law of Peace was translated and written in English (Johansen, 1982).

Under the new law, the blood feud was replaced with the Condolence Ceremony (Grinde, 1977). Indians no longer had the right to avenge a murder by taking the life of the murderer. The victim's family now had to accept strings of wampum from the murderer's family (Grinde, 1977). "The League of the Iroquois arose out of the desire to resolve the problem of the blood feud" (Grinde & Johansen, 2008, p. 28). The Iroquois' constitution put an end to the clan law that required blood revenge (Grinde, 1977). Peace was the goal.

Any decision, such as going to war, had to be unanimous among all the tribes (Johansen, 1982). The chiefs had no power except to persuade. "Indian chiefs would refuse to make decisions without discussing it in council and then gaining approval of most if not all the people" (Grinde, 1977, p. 60). This method of government is time consuming but it encourages widespread participation. "The Iroquois' law and custom upheld freedom of expression in political and religious matters, and it forbade the unauthorized entry of homes" (Johansen, 1982, p. xiv). The League of the Iroquois protected the rights of the people by allowing the people to govern themselves.

How was the League of the Iroquois able to maintain such a system of governance? First, the behavior of individuals was influenced by a strong sense of belonging.

Instead of formal instruments of authority, the Iroquois governed behavior by instilling a sense of pride and belonging to the group through common rituals and the careful rearing of children. Iroquois youth were trained to enter a society that was equalitarian, with power more evenly distributed between male and female, young and old, than was common in Euro-American society. Iroquois culture could be loosely called a "shame culture" because of its emphasis on honor, duty, and collaborative behavior, while European culture was more "guilt-oriented," since it emphasized an authoritarian hierarchy and advancement through the acquisition of property, status, and material possessions.
(Grinde & Johansen, 2008, pp. 27–28)

If the Iroquois failed to do their duty and behave in an honorable fashion, they would feel a strong sense of shame. Another important reason for the success of the League of the Iroquois was their system of checks and balances.

The deliberative process of the League of the Iroquois was designed to ensure that no one was left out of the discussions and that no mistakes were made in their decision. First, the Council of the Mohawks divided into three groups.

116   *A Sense of Belonging*

The third party is to listen only to the discussion of the first and second parties and if an error is made or the proceeding is irregular they are to call attention to it, and when the case is right and properly decided by the two parties they shall confirm the decision of the two parties and refer the case to the Seneca Lords for their decision. When the Seneca Lords have decided in accord with the Mohawk Lords, the case in question shall be referred to the Cayuga and Oneida Lords on the opposite side of the house.

(Grinde, 1977, p. 149)

After the Cayuga and Oneida Lords agreed, the matter was referred to the Onondaga for deliberation and decision (Grinde, 1977). Every tribe had to agree before a decision was reached.

Another component that contributed to the success of the League of Iroquois was that it was designed such that clans overlapped tribal boundaries within the confederacy (Johansen, 1982). "The clan structure and the system of checks and balances kept one nation from seeking to dominate others and helped to insure that consensus would arise from decisions of the council" (Johansen, 1982, pp. 28–29). It was important that people had ties with each other that transcended their tribal nations.

The Europeans and American colonists were very impressed with the culture of the American Indians. "The American Indian was believed to have found many of the answers" (Johansen, 1982, p. 120). Many of the ideas in the Declaration of Independence may have come, at least in part, from Jefferson's views of American Indian society. "The "pursuit of happiness" and the "consent of the governed" were exemplified in Indian polities to which Jefferson…often referred in his writings. The Indian in Jefferson's mind…served as a metaphor for liberty" (Johansen, 1982, p. 102). The "pursuit of happiness" was the primary motivation for Jefferson's proposal for a ward system. The American Indians influenced our culture in many ways.

On September 16, 1987, the Senate of the United States passed Concurrent Resolution 76 to acknowledge the contribution of the Iroquois Confederacy. One clause of the resolution reads: "Whereas the confederation of the original Thirteen Colonies into one republic was explicitly modeled upon the Iroquois Confederacy as were many of the democratic principles which were incorporated into the Constitution itself" (United States Senate, 1987, p. 74). In many ways the Iroquois Confederacy was ahead of its time. Its model of governance is an example of humanity at its best.

C. Wright Mills

Mills' reflections and analysis of the people in modern society lacking a sense of belonging are still relevant today. Mills wrote,

We are losing our sense of belonging because more and more we live in metropolitan areas that are not communities in any real sense of the word….

A Sense of Belonging   117

We do not meet one another as persons in the several aspects of our total life, but know one another only fractionally, as the man who fixes the car, or that girl who serves our lunch, or as the woman who takes care of our child at school. Pre-judgement and prejudice flourish when people meet people only in this segmental manner.

(2008, p. 91)

People rationalize that they are too busy to get to know everyone they routinely encounter. Another explanation is that the way society operates has something to do with this deficit of human interactions.

Mass media, such as television and movies, is the antithesis of face-to-face interaction.

We are losing our sense of belonging because we think that the fabulous techniques of mass communication are not enlarging and animating face-to face public discussion, but are helping to kill it off. These media – radio and mass magazines, television and the movies – as they now generally prevail, increasingly destroy the reasonable and human interchange of opinion. They do not often enable the listener or the viewer truly to connect his daily life with the realities of the world, nor do they often connect with his troubles.

(Mills, 2008, pp. 90–91)

Modern society allows, even encourages, people to keep a distance between themselves. "It is for people in such narrow milieu that the mass media can create a pseudo-world beyond, and a pseudo-world within themselves" (Mills, 2008, p. 91). People are now able to live without a great deal of close human interaction.

How do we come to find ourselves in this situation? It may have to do with how the power structures of modern society operate.

The effective units of power are now the huge corporation, the inaccessible government, the grim military establishment. These centres of power have become larger to the extent that they are effective; and to the extent that they are effective, they have become inaccessible to individuals like us, who would shape by discussion the policies of the organizations to which we belong.

(Mills, 2008, p. 90)

Thus, we have lost the power to influence the organizations that directly affect our daily lives. It is easy for people with no power to become apathetic, disengage with others, and accept the alternative reality of the media. Mills wrote that, "When we say we are losing our sense of belonging we really have in mind a political fact" (2008, p. 90).

By not engaging in face-to-face public discussions, people lose their sense of belonging. This translates into a loss of power for the people, because as Mills wrote,

118 *A Sense of Belonging*

> They [the people] lose their will for decision because they do not possess the means of decision; they lose their sense of political belonging because they do not belong; they lose their political will because they see no way to realize it.
>
> (1958, p. 34)

People need a space where they can engage in deliberations about issues that are important to their lives. An empowered and expanded PB process could provide the space and power needed for people to gain a sense of belonging.

Julien Talpin

The character of the people determines the extent of their involvement with government.[1] "People have understood – some of them centuries ago – that the quality of a democracy largely stems from the quality of its citizenry. Non-participation and apathy are no longer seen as optimally functional for a democracy" (Talpin, 2011, p. xii).[2] Recall from Chapter 6, the Port Huron Statement saw participatory democracy as a way to fight apathy and effect social change. "One of the expected benefits of local participation – for both elected officials and political theorists – is indeed the nurturing of a competent citizenry" (Talpin, 2011, p. 2). These are citizens who take an interest in, and work toward, making things better.

As noted in Chapter 3, Talpin conducted ethnographic research of three European PB processes. "Having conducted comparative ethnographic studies over 18 months in three participatory democracy institutions in different southern European cities, I [Talpin] managed to follow the trajectory of some participants over time.... I [Talpin] saw some of them changing" (Talpin, 2011, p. xx). Talpin was able to gain some insight into why some participants changed as a result of the PB process.

The three PB processes, in Talpin's research, are Morsang-sur-Orgie, France, Rome Municipo XI, Italy, and Seville, Spain (Talpin, 2011). "These cases have been chosen as they embody three of the most ambitious PB experiences in Europe, devolving an important decision-making power to citizens" (Talpin, 2011, p. xvii). Per Mills analysis in the previous section, these are most likely to give participants a strong sense of belonging since they have more decision-making power. Thus, these PB processes could be facilitating the greatest amount of change in participants, at least in Europe.

Talpin wrote that, "Participation in the public sphere could have deep transformative effects on individuals" (2011, p. 1). To explain self-change within the PB process Talpin uses the publicity hypothesis and the emotional hypothesis (Talpin, 2011) "made conceptually coherent through a pragmatist epistemology and concepts such as the 'grammar of public life'" (2011, p. 14).[3] To be taken seriously participants had to use the correct grammar for their PB process. Their speech needed to include reference to the common-good, be non-political, and appear to be practical (Talpin, 2011). "Grammars ... are therefore derived from the implicit or explicit consensus between actors on the right and wrong moves in certain situations" (Talpin, 2011, p. 22). Talpin found that grammars were enforced by shaming the rule-breakers.

Part of Talpin's pragmatist perspective is taking preferences as endogenous. "Preferences are thus not pre-political or fixed, but instead, the changing product of social interaction. The goal of deliberation is therefore precisely the formation or discovery of one's preferences (Manin 1987)" (Talpin, 2011, p. 16). Preferences can be shaped and clarified during deliberation.

The publicity hypothesis is about how being in public changes the way we talk. "Inspired by Kantian philosophy, the publicity hypothesis puts the emphasis on the power of publicity to filter people's selfish motives and to induce individuals to present themselves as oriented towards the common good" (Talpin, 2011, p. 10). People care about how others think about them.

The emotional hypothesis is about the emotions of face-to-face relationships. "The theory of social capital can indeed be summed up in a short formula: relationships matter" (Taplin, 2011, p. 10). Relationships matter because they are emotional.[4]

Since PB is all about face-to-face relationships, it makes sense to look at Putnam's social capital. "Trust, reciprocity and solidarity are supposed to stem from face-to-face interaction (Putnam 1993; 1995)" (Talpin, 2011, p. 13). These characteristics of social interaction are all consistent with an increased sense of belonging. The next section takes a closer look at Putnam's social capital.

The Social Capital of Robert Putnam

The concept of social capital has been controversial. But, a well-run PB process does seem to have social capital. First, there is not one generally accepted definition of social capital. This is partly due to social capital being composed of several social phenomena. Secondly, it is controversial because social capital does not meet all of the traditional criteria of being capital. It is beyond the scope of this monograph to comment on the validity of social capital outside of the PB process. However, Putnam's description of social capital does seem to fit the dynamics of a well-run PB process. It might be that a well-run PB process provides a unique environment that combines civil society, the state, and direct democracy where deliberation can occur in public assemblies and where individuals are empowered to make decisions. Participants can begin to think of themselves of part of the community and experience a sense of belonging, as opposed to isolated individuals. Thus, at least for the PB process, the generation of social capital and a sense of belonging seem to be inexorably tied together.

This section begins with a brief examination of the history of the social capital concept. Then, the capital debate controversy of social capital is addressed. The next subsection will review Putnam's understanding of social capital and why Putnam's idea of social capital seems to work in the PB process.

120   *A Sense of Belonging*

History of Social Capital

There are various definitions of social capital, which are reviewed in this section. "The commonality of most definitions is that they emphasize social relations that generate productive benefits" (Bhandari & Yasunobu, 2009, p. 487). More specifically, when social networks are used, the benefits of social capital are created by the relationships of the people participating in the networks, such as increased trust, which can result in increased productivity, both economic and social. "The idea of social capital can be traced long back but its entry into academic and policy debates can be credited to the pioneering work of Pierre Bourdieu (1986), James Coleman (1988) and Robert Putnam (1993)" (Bhandari & Yasunobu, 2009, p. 487). The work of these three social scientists is briefly reviewed. "The dominating paradigm in the current literature on social capital is largely based on Coleman's (1988) definition and on the work of Putnam (1995)" (Poder, 2011, p. 350).

Putnam was not the first to use the concept. However, he did play "a prominent role in popularizing the concept of social capital" (Bhandari & Yasunobu, 2009, p. 488), through publication of *Making Democracy Work* (1994) and *Bowling Alone* (2000). Putnam's approach to social capital seems to have resonated better than those of other authors.

> Robert Putnam is undoubtedly the author who has done more to popularize the concept of social capital both inside and outside academic circles. His theory – or his speech – is based largely on the concept of social capital by Coleman (1988, 1990) and little on the sociology of networks.
>
> (Poder, 2011, p. 348)

A general definition that seems to include all the social phenomena discussed in the literature of social capital is:

> Social capital is broadly defined to be a multidimensional phenomenon encompassing a stock of social norms, values, beliefs, trusts, obligations, relationships, networks, friends, memberships, civic engagement, information flows, and institutions that foster cooperation and collective actions for mutual benefits and contributes to economic and social development.
>
> (Bhandari & Yasunobu, 2009, p. 486)

Some of these social phenomena are consistent with a sense of belonging.

As was noted, there is not a single definition of social capital. "The main difference between these definitions is that they treat social capital as either personal resources or social resources" (Bhandari & Yasunobu, 2009, p. 487). Bourdieu sees social capital as an individual good that is acquired from group membership. "It [social capital] is a personal asset in the competition among individuals aiming to improve their own positions as compared to others" (Bhandari & Yasunobu, 2009, p. 488). The quantity of an individual's social capital depends on the size of the social networks of which they are members, and the amount of social capital owned by members within these networks (Bourdieu, 1986). Bourdieu defines social capital as "the aggregate of the actual or potential resources that are linked to the possession of a durable network of more or less institutional relationships of mutual acquaintance and recognition – in other words, to membership in a group" (Bourdieu, 1986, p. 248).

"For Coleman, social capital is a public good as it exists in the relations among people" (Bhandari & Yasunobu, 2009, p. 488). Coleman believed it was not an individual good because it could only be created and maintained in human interactions. "Coleman identifies three forms of social capital: reciprocity (including trust), information channels and flow of information, and norms enforced by sanction" (Bhandari & Yasunobu, 2009, p. 488). The reciprocity form "means that obligations will be repaid" (Coleman, 1988, p. S102). Information channels are critical to determine action. "An important form of social capital is the potential for information that inheres [is inherent] in social relations" (Coleman, 1988, p. S104). And norms prescribe behavior that benefits the group. "When a norm exists and is effective, it constitutes a powerful, though sometimes fragile, form of social capital" (Coleman, 1988, p. S104). Coleman believed that all human interactions contributed toward social capital. In 1988, Coleman wrote, "All social relations and social structures facilitate some forms of social capital" (p. S105).

Putnam, in *Making Democracy Work*, wrote: "Social capital here refers to features of social organizations, such as trust, norms, and networks, that can improve the efficiency of society by facilitating actions.... Spontaneous cooperation is facilitated by social capital" (1994, p. 167). Putnam believed that social capital can increase the productivity of both individuals and groups (Putnam, 2000).

Capital Debate Controversy of Social Capital

There is some controversy whether social capital should be defined as capital. How do capital goods compare with social capital?

> Several authors have clearly pointed out the weaknesses of the analogy between physical capital and social capital. Arrow (2000) argues that physical capital has three important characteristics: extension in time, deliberate sacrifice in the present for future benefits, and alienability (transfer of ownership from one person to another). To him, social capital shares only the time dimension aspect with physical capital (for example, trust or reputation take some time to develop); but it does not necessarily require any material sacrifice; in most cases it is also difficult to transfer the ownership of social capital from one person to another.
>
> (Bhandari & Yasunobu, 2009, p. 493)

Of course, there are clearly differences between tangible capital goods and intangible social capital.

122   *A Sense of Belonging*

It may help to more closely examine why social capital does not meet Arrow's second characteristic of physical capital, deliberate sacrifice in the present for future benefits. It seems to depend on motivations and the definition of sacrifice. Social capital does not necessarily require any material sacrifice. However, it does require a sacrifice of one's time. Also, the motivation of people joining associations might be to connect with other people, instead of a calculation of time sacrificed for the sake of future personal enrichment. Robison, Schmid, and Siles questioned, "Is there a contradiction between individual or collective investment in social capital that implies calculation and the emotive non-calculating response of persons for persons?" (2002, p. 15). It does not seem like motivations should matter.

Money is required to start and run a PB process, and the future benefits would include distributing public goods and services in a more fair and transparent manner, which might be expected to reduce costs, such as corruption. Benefits would also include providing people with a sense of community and a sense of belonging. Of course, a benefit to local politicians who support a popular social innovation would be votes.

Arrow's third characteristic of social capital is alienability (transfer of ownership from one person to another). There are situations in which the owner of social capital may transfer ownership. "For example, friends of my parents may become my friends because of the efforts of my parents. A baby who is born into a particular social structure and in particular to a family may immediately 'own' social capital" (Robison et al., 2002, p. 16). However, social capital cannot be sold or rented. The social capital received from a PB process also cannot be sold or rented. However, everyone in the community would be encouraged to attend and participate in PB assemblies. Thus, the social capital received from PB seems to meet some – but not all – of the characteristics of capital.

The main idea of social capital is that networks of people can experience increased cooperation, which increases productivity. Putnam wrote:

> [T]he core idea of social capital theory is that social networks have value. Just as a screwdriver (physical capital) or a college education (human capital) can increase productivity (both individual and collective), so too social contacts affect the productivity of individuals and groups.
>
> (2000, pp. 18–19)

Thus, it seems clear that human interactions can facilitate cooperation which affects both the individual and the community. Is it a type of capital?

> The term social capital is now firmly entrenched in the language of social scientists. Thus, for now and some considerable time in the future, the term "social capital" will be in common use among most social scientists, if not most economists, and the task will be to make the most of it.
>
> (Robison et al., 2002, p. 8)

This research monograph accepts the term social capital.

Putnam's Social Capital

Putnam believes that social capital improves the efficacy, or productivity, of society by facilitating cooperation. In 2000, Putnam wrote, "social capital refers to connections among individuals – social networks and the norms of reciprocity and trustworthiness that arise from them" (p. 39). Putnam believes there are two types of social capital:

> "Bonding capital," consisting of homogeneous groups with much in common who develop trust and reciprocal relationships; and "bridging capital," involving heterogeneous groups, typically with divergent views and different demographics who nevertheless develop generalized trust. It is argued that the latter networks, "bridging capital," are more likely to produce these positive social outcomes than bonding capital.
>
> (Wampler & Hartz-Karp, 2012, p. 2)

Putnam wrote, "Bonding social capital (as distinct from bridging social capital) is particularly likely to have illiberal effects" (2000, p. 358). Discrimination may result from bonding social capital. "The civil rights movement was, in part, aimed at destroying certain exclusive, nonbridging forms of social capital – racially homogeneous schools, neighborhoods, and so forth" (Putnam, 2000, p. 362).

Having too much bonding capital is a real danger for PB processes as Wampler and Hartz-Karp write about in a special issue of *Journal of Public Deliberation*, which focused on PB.

> Since most PB initiatives researched have relied upon civic organizations with common objectives developing a proposal together, more or less in competition for scarce resources with other civic organizations, it is more likely that bonding capital is being enhanced than bridging capital.
>
> (2012, p. 2)

This tendency can be reversed with active recruitment of typically marginalized groups of people to participate in the PB process.

The social relationships formed in the PB process could provide the passion needed for individuals to change their mindsets and begin thinking of themselves as part of the community. We need to know how the PB process is sometimes able to provide an environment where this metamorphosis can occur.

In 2003, Baiocchi completed an ethnographic investigation of two Porto Alegre districts to discover how the PB process contributed to the transformation from "I" to "we." One district had a strong civic society and the other did not. Baiocchi wrote, "it is clear from Porto Alegre that state-sponsored institutions have proven important in fostering open-ended discussions in unlikely settings" (2003, p. 68). They were unlikely settings because they were poor districts where people might not be expected to be able to engage in "civic discourse and deliberation" (p. 68). By open-ended discussions, Baiocchi meant discussions that

124   *A Sense of Belonging*

went "beyond the stated purpose of the meetings, which was to allocate budget priorities" (2003, p. 53). People got caught up in discussing policies that affected their community.

Sometimes these open-ended discussions resulted in a meeting being taken over by a non-agenda topic. These non-agenda topics were usually introduced at the beginning of the meeting in time that had been allocated for announcements (Baiocchi, 2003). During the announcements time, "many often took the opportunity to share news, events, and other items deemed relevant to community life" (Baiocchi, 2003, p. 60). Thus, even though the facilitators set the agenda, sometimes the participants determined what was to be discussed. "The discussion of a specific 'news' issue sometimes became a discussion of politics and economics, government policy, or macroeconomic problems, not to mention specific community problems" (Baiocchi, 2003, p. 60).

People in these assemblies used a "language of citizenship" which "emphasized 'the good of the community' and valued collective and pragmatic problem-solving" (Baiocchi, 2003, p. 62). Participants were able to link private needs to public problems (Baiocchi, 2003). Baiocchi reported in 2003 that as a result of this type of approach to problem-solving, "Participants often mentioned a sense of belonging to a larger community of citizens who together are facing problems together, as a result of having worked together over the year to decide on projects" (p. 62). This sense of belonging is what creates a community. It is another way to describe social capital. Baiocchi found that the state's role in PB was critical to its success. He wrote that "interviews showed that it was difficult to establish such public-minded discussions on a regular basis in settings outside of the state-sponsored institutions" (2003, p. 66). The state is able to provide access to information, experts within city agencies, and a space to deliberate.

The role of civic society in PB was also examined in this ethnographic study.

> The social networks in Por-do-Sol were important, not so much in turning an "I into We," (Putnam, 1995), but in preventing the "We" of the discussions on collective projects from turning into an "I" of personal disputes as happened in Nazare.
>
> (Baiocchi, 2003, p. 69)

The Por-do-Sol district had an established civic society prior to the introduction of PB, while Nazare did not (Baiocchi, 2003). The presence of an established civic society means that community activists have more experience. Baiocchi wrote,

> experienced activists and well-developed civic networks prevented these open-ended discussions from becoming too disruptive or too personal.... Because this [PB assembly] was essentially the only meeting place for the whole community and the Nazare community lacked experienced participants who could maintain order, these interruptions and digressions more often derailed meetings altogether.
>
> (2003, p. 53)

A Sense of Belonging   125

Baiocchi's investigation also found that PB expands civic society organizations.[5] Baiocchi wrote, "these budget assemblies have fostered significant forms of civic engagement throughout the city" (2003, p. 69). Civic society and the PB process seem to have a symbiotic relationship.

The ability of PB to connect private needs to public policy is an evolution of how Mills and the Port Huron Statement envisioned it. Mills believed it was the duty of social scientists to translate personal needs into public issues, in order to provide publics with relevant issues. As was noted in the previous chapter, the Port Huron Statement, in the 1960s, this task was accomplished with consciousness-raising groups. Now, it seems, this duty can be performed in well-run PB assemblies where people actively participate.

Notes

1 In Chapter 6, Emerson made the argument that governments originate in the morality of men.
2 See Chapter 1, in the arguments against PB section, for a description of the argument that apathy is good.
3 Grammar was discussed in Chapter 3, in the recommendations for communicative dimension section.
4 Dewey also believed that emotions can interrupt habitual ways of thinking and possibly lead to new ways of acting (see Chapter 1).
5 The expansion of civic society organizations was more pronounced in areas that already had an established civic society.

References

Baiocchi, G. (2003). Emergent public spheres: Talking politics in participatory govern-ance. *American Sociological Review, 68*(1), 52–74.
Bhandari, H., & Yasunobu, K. (2009). What is social capital? A comprehensive review of the concept. *Asian Journal of Social Sciences, 37*(3), 480–510.
Bourdieu, P. (1986). The forms of capital. In J. Richardson (Ed.), *Handbook of theory and research for the sociology of education* (pp. 241–258), Westport, CT: Greenwood Press.
Coleman, J. (1988). Social capital in the creation of human capital. *The American Journal of Sociology, 94*(Supplement), S95–S120.
Grinde, D. (1977). *The Iroquois and the founding of the American nation.* USA: The Indian Historical Press.
Grinde, D., & Johansen, B. (2008). *Exemplar of liberty: Native America and the evolution of democracy* (2nd ed.). Los Angeles, CA: American Indian Studies Center.
Jefferson, T. (2011). *Jefferson writings* (M. Peterson, Ed.). New York: Penguin Group.
Johansen, B. (1982). *Forgotten founders: How the American Indian helped shape demo-cracy.* Cambridge, MA: The Harvard Common Press.
Mills, C. W. (1958). *The causes of World War Three.* New York: Simon and Schuster.
Mills, C. W. (2008). *The politics of truth: Selected writings of C. Wright Mills.* New York: Oxford University Press.
Poder, T. (2011). What is really social capital? A critical review. *The American Sociolo-gist, 42*(4), 341–367.

126   *A Sense of Belonging*

Putnam, R. (1994). *Making democracy work: Civic traditions in modern Italy* (5th ed.). Princeton, NJ: Princeton University Press.

Putnam, R. (2000). *Bowling alone*. New York: Simon & Schuster Paperbacks.

Robison, L., Schmid, A., & Siles, M. (2002). Is social capital really capital? *Review of Social Economy, 60*(1), 1–21.

Talpin, J. (2011). *Schools of democracy*. Colchester, UK: European Consortium for Political Research.

United States Senate. (1987). S. CON. RES. 76. In J. Barreiro (Ed.), *Indian roots of American democracy* (pp. 74–75). USA: Northeast Indian Quarterly.

Wampler, B., & Hartz-Karp, J. (2012). Participatory budgeting: Diffusion and outcomes across the world. *Journal of Public Deliberation, 8*(2), article 13.

8   Conclusion

This research is not just about democracy; it is about the quality of democracy. It is the conclusion of this research that approaching the highest quality of democracy by providing training for public deliberation, having trained facilitators, and using direct social action to further empower and expand PB into local direct democracies will improve the life of participants and improve the well-being of communities. This is needed now because the alternative mentioned in Chapter 1 is the worldwide trend of far right authoritarian leaders who attack democratic norms and institutions for the sake of their own and their party's political power. First, it may help to briefly review why democracy has been so popular around the world in modern times. Next, the current trend of far right authoritarian leaders is reviewed. Then, the alternative presented in this research monograph is reviewed.

Giving people the chance to make their own decisions is probably the best reason for the popularity of democracy. Also, there are logical reasons for democratic governance.

> The strongest point to be made in behalf of even such rudimentary political forms as democracy has already attained, popular voting, majority rule and so on, is that to some extent they involve a consultation and discussion which uncover social needs and troubles.
>
> (Dewey, 1954, p. 206)

The democratic process is a good way to discover what is most needed.

The democratic process, at both the national and local levels, have pragmatic benefits. In *Development as Freedom*, Sen wrote,

> No substantial famine has ever occurred in any independent country with a democratic form of government and a relatively free press. Famines have occurred in ancient kingdoms and contemporary authoritarian societies, in primitive tribal communities and in modern technocratic dictatorships, in colonial economies run by imperialists from the north and in newly independent countries of the south run by despotic national leaders or by intolerant single parties.
>
> (Sen, 2001, pp. 152–153)

128 *Conclusion*

This points to the value that the democratic process places on human life. "In a democracy, people tend to get what they demand, and more crucially, do not typically get what they do not demand" (Sen, 2001, p. 155). Of course, no one wants a famine.

At the local level, the case of Flint, Michigan was reviewed in Chapter 1. For the sake of economic expediency, an emergency manager was appointed to Flint with the power to make all economic decisions in order to place the town on sound economic footing (Kossis, 2012). Evidently, the thinking was that the economic solutions were well known; and, it was just the burden of the time-consuming democratic process that was preventing Flint, and other towns, from doing the right thing. Well, the emergency manager changed the source of the town's water supply to save money. The result was that the water was acidic, corroded the lead water pipes, and was poisoning the people with lead (Bosman, Davey, & Smith, 2016). It is likely that any democratic process would have insisted on extensive testing of the water before exposing their children to it.

It seems clear that a democracy may avoid crisis situations, such as famine at the national level or unsafe drinking water at the local level, which other forms of governance are not able to avoid. The people should be allowed to demand that which is most important to them. This is how democracy benefits the people.

However, what is happening within democracies now is far different from what one might read in a civics textbook. As documented in Chapter 1, the authoritarian leaders attack the free press, independent judges, immigrants, racial minorities, rights of women, and cultural minorities. These leaders attack multi-culturalism by using prejudice and discrimination (Gogoi, 2009; Golder, 2016; Norris & Inglehart, 2019). They use political rhetoric to misrepresent minorities, such as immigrants, to invoke fear and hatred for the purpose of political power at the expense of human rights. The far right leaders and their political parties do not want to belong to supranational governance organizations, such as the EU, because the international organizations may pass laws protecting human rights for all human beings, that member states would be required to follow. The far right authoritarian leaders and their parties would prefer to keep all their options available (Drolet, 2010). Although the far right authoritarian leaders do not declare that they are against democracy, their actions do not indicate a great deal of respect for democracy.

Many democracies around the world are broken. The proof is the trend of far right authoritarian parties gaining power. I submit that part of the cause are the political parties who seem to be more concerned with their own political power than of the welfare of the people. The parties seem to be the ones who benefit from the political chaos.

For example, the Republican party of the United States is an example of seeking political power at the expense of the smooth functioning of government. The roots of the current political polarization of politics in the United States can be traced back to Newt Gingrich, who became the House Speaker during the Clinton presidency (Mann & Ornstein, 2016). Gingrich sought "to unite his Republicans in refusing to cooperate with Democrats in committee and on the

Conclusion 129

floor, while publicly attacking them as a permanent majority presiding over and benefiting from a thoroughly corrupt institution" (Mann & Ornstein, 2016, p. 33). Of course, compromise is critical to ensure the political system functions smoothly. "He [Gingrich] was able to convince his party to vote en masse against major Clinton initiatives" (Mann & Ornstein, 2016, p. 39). But perhaps one of the most divisive practices promoted by Gingrich was the social separation of politicians in Washington D. C. based on party membership. "At the urging of Gingrich and other leaders, most [elected Republican politicians] left their families in their districts and spent as little time in Washington as possible" (Mann & Ornstein, 2016, p. 40). This prevented politicians from getting to know their fellow politicians in the other party. It is much easier to demonize and refuse to compromise with people you do not know. Of course, by forcing legislators to vote strictly along party lines, no real deliberations were taking place. The only deliberation taking place was among the party leaders who decided what their party was going to vote for or against. One of the keys to making democracy work was the understanding that the representatives of the people would honestly debate legislation in a public forum. Now, the only real debating, and deal-making, is behind closed doors among a very few in leadership. "The parties have become ideologically polarized, tribalized, and strategically partisan" (Mann & Ornstein, 2012, p. xiv). The parties seem to be more focused on their own welfare than the welfare of the people.

The downgrading of democracies around the world seems to be happening slowly.

> Last year, the downgrading of the United States from a "full democracy" to a "flawed democracy" in the annual Democracy Index by Economist Intelligence Unit made waves across international media. Although many commentators rushed to point to the election of Donald Trump as the determinant factor of this decline, the report insists this was not a cause but a result of it.
>
> (Del Valle Ruiz, 2017, p. 161)

There does not seem to be any one event or any one person responsible for the erosion of the quality of democracy.

> Popular wisdom states that if you toss a frog into a pot of boiling water, the creature will jump right out and try to escape. However, if you slowly turn up the heat of the water when the frog is already in it, by the time it realizes the danger, it is too late to jump. The story may yet prove to be a relevant parable for democracy.
>
> (Del Valle Ruiz, 2017, p. 170)

The question is do we sit back and do nothing; or, do we take action?

The action proposed in this research monograph is not only to circumvent the political parties, but to create municipal direct democracies that can act as a

130　*Conclusion*

check to the monopoly power that parties have over politics by following these incremental steps. First, PB should break ties with political parties, which has been shown to be necessary with the example of PB in Porto Alegre, Brazil (Baiocchi & Ganuza, 2017), in Chapter 1. Secondly, even though PB, or eventually the municipal direct democracies, have no authority beyond local issues they may pass nonbinding resolutions on anything they feel strongly about, which has seemed to work in the United States (Bookchin, 1995) (see Chapter 1). And lastly, if politicians ignore the nonbinding resolutions, these local democracies could vote to peaceably protest unjust situations. I believe that even an authoritarian leader would have to stand up and take notice if enough people took to the streets to protest something he had done.

Another way improved and expanded PB processes, or local direct democracies, could influence state and federal governments is that the people becoming the local government will feel reinvigorated and are likely to become more involved in their state and federal governments (see Chapter 4). Then, the state and federal governments will be revitalized as more people take more active roles in the higher levels of governments (Koch, 1964).

This research has shown that it is possible to experience the democratic ideal. The League of the Iroquois, as explained in Chapter 7, were living the deliberative democratic ideal, with an oral constitution, when settlers landed in the New England area of North America. This confederation of tribes had developed their skills at public deliberation to the point where they were able to govern themselves by consensus. Their example helped the founding fathers of the United States to formulate and articulate the democratic norms and principles into the Constitution of the United States (United States Senate, 1987). The American Indians also seem to have inspired Thomas Jefferson to include the phrase 'pursuit of happiness' as one of the unalienable rights in the Declaration of Independence (Matthews, 1986).

It is likely that American Indians also inspired Jefferson's ward system proposal, which is reviewed in Chapter 4. Jefferson admired the way that American Indian tribes were able to live in peace and without coercive government (Jefferson, 2011), which confirmed Jefferson's belief in people. After he retired from being the President of the United States, Jefferson proposed in letters to several people (Jefferson, 2011) that the country be divided into wards. Each ward would be small enough so that everyone who lived within the ward could meet in one place to make decisions about local issues such as schools, road maintenance, police protection, fire protection, and care for the poor (Jefferson, 2011). These local democracies, or wards, could provide individuals the chance to become the government. People participating in local direct democracies will experience public happiness. Government will no longer be something the people need to be protected from once the people become the government.

It seems significant that one of the founding fathers of the United States was the first to recognize that something fundamental was missing from the political system of the United States. Jefferson knew the people needed a public space for participation that would help ensure their freedom and happiness (Arendt, 2006).

Conclusion 131

Such a public space could reinvigorate the people and help keep the revolutionary spirit alive. Expanded, empowered, and deliberative PB processes could create public happiness and a passion for democracy. Otherwise, if we give up our right to public happiness, we also give up our right to power. The political leaders take that power that was not claimed by the people (Arendt, 2006).

Democracy could become a way of life. As people see the improvements in themselves and their communities, they most likely will devote more time and energy participating. Individuals may reorder their priorities and focus on the activities that allow them and their communities to flourish. Perhaps, it is now time for the United States to continue its tradition of democratic innovation by empowering people at the local level. This could reinvigorate individuals and our political system.

There has been a narrative that people must choose between individualism and society, or between individuals and the state. Whitman understood that for a democratic government to function best, there needed to be a reconciliation between that individual and society (see Chapter 6). In "Democratic Vistas" he wrote about the need for individuals to support society and vice versa. During his time (around the American civil war), Whitman felt "their oppositions form a serious problem and paradox" (1982, p. 941). Whitman anticipated that this reconciliation would benefit both the individual and society as well as producing additional benefits.

On the other hand, Dewey (mid-twentieth century) felt that there was no conflict between individuals and the state (Chapter 2). He saw the development of the individual as the solution to the ethical problem of the individual to the state. Public face-to-face communication serves the dual purpose of helping individuals and as well as helping the community because the individual will approach realizing their full capacities as they participate (Dewey, 1993). Thus, there is no conflict between the interests of a community and the interests of an individual. The additional benefits that Whitman believed would occur could be a virtuous cycle of individuals realizing the benefits of participation, then increasing their participation, which creates additional benefits for the community and for participants, which would further increase participation, and so on.

People will learn that they can make their own decisions without political parties and without experts having the final say. Relying on experts can result in bureaucrats making decisions whose primary concerns do not match with the people. Relying on the political parties exposes everyone to the daily political rhetoric of lies, misrepresentations, and hatred that politicians use to differentiate themselves from their opponents, which creates mistrust and division among citizens. It also exposes us to the gridlock and political games used to gain and maintain power. Also, it seems to lead to authoritarian leaders gaining power. An empowered people engaging in local well-run public deliberations could be the best antidote for the political parties because people will discover they can debate and decide political issues on their own. Cooperation could become the method we use to get things done.

132 *Conclusion*

Based on the experience of PBNYC, deliberative researchers, and Foster's theory of institutional adjustment (Chapter 2) recommendations are made, in Chapter 3, that should allow PBNYC to realize the intangible benefits of an ideal democracy, as stated in the hypothesis. The recommendations are grouped into the communicative and political dimensions of PB. The political dimension of PB refers to the extent that the PB process is empowered to make decisions. The other aspect of the political dimension is expanding PB to include more responsibilities and more funding. An empowered PB process means that participants can make decisions without bureaucratic agencies being able to arbitrarily change or overrule their decisions. A PB process is empowered when the city's administrative structure is reorganized so that PB is above the other municipal bureaucracies in the administrative hierarchy. This will embed PB in the municipal administration and prevent other bureaucracies' priorities from interfering with PB decisions. And the expansion of the PB process will likely encourage more people to participate. Both of these political aspects can be accomplished with the help of a united group of civic organizations, which can help mobilize the people to peaceably demand these changes be made. Civic groups will be motivated to help because local direct democracies will most likely prioritize many of the same things as the civic groups.

The reason changes are needed in the communicative dimension is that many people may not know how to publically deliberate. Training needs to be available for everyone in the process. Because, to participate effectively people should know how to deliberate.

The face-to-face deliberative aspect of PB will help people better understand each other, as explained in Chapter 5. In order to be more effective deliberators participants may need to work at keeping an open mind. This will help individuals better understand the subjective experiences of others, which Schutz's research (Chapter 5) showed is possible. Dewey's philosophy reminds us of the importance of understanding one another. And Mills' reasoning offers an explanation of why modern society tends to cultivate a generalized lack of understanding throughout society. Mills' solution was for small groups of individuals to discuss the issues that were most important to them. By understanding each other's problems, they could then link them to policy issues. Working groups within the PB process could satisfy Mills' requirements.

The way to achieve all the potential benefits, which are reviewed in this study, is to work toward implementing the proposed changes. This is not a quick and easy fix, even if the monetary cost is not considered. For example, going to classes to learn how to publically deliberate will take a commitment of time and energy. It will take work for people to reflect on what they believe and then be able to publically defend their positions. And people may need to work at developing the discipline to keep an open mind, which means really listening to other people and being ready and willing to modify one's positions, in the light of new information or new arguments. Also, part of the recommendations for public deliberations is that they be monitored and evaluated with an eye to continuously improving the process.

Conclusion 133

The political dimension will be difficult as well. But motivated individuals can find the time to commit to a worthy cause. People joining together in peaceful protests to demand that local authorities restructure the municipal bureaucratic hierarchy to fully empower a local direct democracy, expand its responsibilities, and provide training for public deliberation will form bonds of friendship and solidarity. The people will learn about civic engagement, civic responsibility, and local governance by living it.

Individuals working together on a variety of policy issues can transform themselves and their communities as participants increasingly gain a sense of belonging, as explained in Chapter 7. Mills' analysis explains how modern society makes individuals feel powerless and isolated. He interpreted our loss of a sense of belonging to be a loss of a political sense of belonging. An empowered and expanded PBNYC will empower the powerless and create community for the isolated.

Talpin learned how some individuals' lives were transformed by studying the three European PB processes that gave participants the most decision-making authority. Talpin believed that part of the reason for the transformation was that people in public try to put themselves in the best light and talk about the common good. Another part of the reason why some people were transformed, according to Talpin, was due to the emotions of face-to-face relationships, which can transform people with a sense of belonging, trust, and solidarity. Talpin thought that emotions were what Putnam's social capital was all about (Talpin, 2011). It turns out that people in well-run PB assemblies create social capital simultaneously with creating a sense of belonging among participants (Baiocchi, 2003) (see Chapter 7). It can bring greater meaning into participant's lives by creating the opportunity to serve and help the community. By helping others, we can help ourselves.

The combination of public deliberation and non-violent direct social action could spark the imagination of people. As more people become better at deliberating local issues and making decisions with others, individuals will become empowered and discover their better selves. People will realize they can help make things better. As people work with one another to improve their communities their morality will develop and tend to converge, per the social philosophers in Chapter 6. Just as the Port Huron Statement (PHS) inspired social movements in the sixties (see Chapter 6) an empowered, deliberative, and expanded PBNYC process could inspire people to recreate the PBNYC process across the United States and around the world.

It could be said that the 1960s Cultural Revolution, in the United States, was incomplete since the primary theme of the Port Huron Statement (participatory democracy) was never integrated into the United States political system. The empowered, deliberative, and local direct democracies proposed in this monograph is one way to implement participatory democracy within the existing representative political system. Thus, it could be said that this research monograph's proposal is to complete the Cultural Revolution of the 1960s.

Had participatory democracy been integrated into the political system in the 1960s, it would have provided a public forum where views about immigration,

134   *Conclusion*

race, sexual minorities, abortion, and other issues could have been talked about. Well-run public forums would enable people to better understand one another. Participants could have been exposed to different facts and arguments which may have altered their positions. Public deliberation tends to bring different viewpoints closer to each other. Extreme viewpoints would be hard to try to justify and would likely be modified. People would see their political opponents as human beings, which would make it harder to demonize them.

It is ironic that the rise of authoritarian leaders may be due, in part, to an incomplete Cultural Revolution of the 1960s. If participatory democracy had been created in the 1960s and widely used, most of what authoritarian leaders campaign on today would most likely be laughed at. Instead of allowing political leaders to inflame the cultural issues for the purpose of political power, people would be able to talk face-to-face with people who have different points of view. In deliberative public forums, people could talk about these and other issues without name-calling or yelling and the extreme views would tend to move closer to each other as people came to understand one another. People may then come to realize that others with different viewpoints may have good reason for holding the views that they do. The same is true for the different minority groups of people that authoritarian leaders use to spread fear and hatred among the general population. Once participants talk with people from these groups, they would soon realize that they are just people just like everyone else

The authoritarian leaders use words like traditional morality and traditional culture to justify discrimination and worse. The truth is that helping other human beings is the most noble and sacred of our traditions. The saddest thing is that by accepting politicians' lies, people are depriving themselves of the joy of being free of hate and being free of fear. And by not standing up to these lies they are participating in hurting others.

Self-reflection is the key to change. As reviewed in Chapter 1, self-reflection can be provoked by emotions which interrupt habitual ways of thinking and acting. It can then lead to changing habitual ways of thinking and acting. This could happen during deliberations in public forums. It could happen as people consciously reflect on what is most important in their lives. And self-reflection could be provoked by the anger of what the political leaders are saying and doing. Self-reflection proceeds change.

We should allow ourselves to believe in a vision of how life can be better. The capacity to aspire is a precondition for people to improve their lives (Appadurai, 2004). All the social philosophers in this monograph contribute to that vision. As Thoreau would say, if you believe in something you owe it to yourself and to others to act on it (1996). We can all be a part of the next stage in democracy (Whitman, 1982), if we allow ourselves to be inspired by the possibilities. Do we march to the tune of authoritarian leaders; or, do we work to get rid of fear and hatred and replace it with understanding, happiness, a higher morality, and a sense of belonging to a community?

This research monograph starts with a great social innovation (PB) based on an ideal of democracy then proposes to support it with training in public deliberation,

Conclusion 135

proposes to build broad civic support for it, and proposes to expand it to encompass the city. The purpose is to spark the imagination and rekindle the democratic revolutionary spirit. This is needed because democracies have been corrupted by big business, big money, and small politicians. It may be time to rediscover the benefits of a real democracy.

References

Appadurai, A. (2004). The capacity to aspire: Culture and the terms of recognition. In V. Rao & M. Walton (Eds.), *Culture and public action* (pp. 59–84), Stanford, CA: Stanford University Press.

Arendt, H. (2006). *On revolution* (4th ed.). New York: Penguin Books.

Baiocchi, G. (2003). Emergent public spheres: Talking politics in participatory governance. *American Sociological Review*, *68*(1), 52–74.

Baiocchi, G., & Ganuza, E. (2017). *Popular democracy: The paradox of participation.* Stanford, CA: Stanford University Press.

Bookchin, M. (1995). *From urbanization to cities: Toward a new politics of citizenship* (2nd ed.). London: Cassell.

Bosman, J., Davey, M., & Smith, S. (2016, January 21). As water problems grew, officials belittled complaints from Flint. *The New York Times*. Retrieved from www. nytimes.com/2016/01/21/us/flint-michigan-lead-water-crisis.html?_r=0

Del Valle Ruiz, Á. (2017). The slow death of western democracy and what happens after. *Journal of International Affairs*, *71*(1), 161–174.

Dewey, J. (1954). *The public and its problems*. Athens, Ohio: Swallow Press/Ohio University Press Books.

Dewey, J. (1993). The ethics of democracy. In D. Morris & I. Shapiro (Eds.), *John Dewey: The political writings* (pp. 59–65). Indianapolis, IN: Hackett Publishing Company.

Drolet, J. (2010). Containing the Kantian revolutions: A theoretical analysis of the neoconservative critique of global liberal governance. *Review of International Studies*, *36*, 533–560.

Gogoi, P. (2019, January 21). Analysis: How the rise of the far right threatens democracy worldwide. Retrieved from www.npr.org/2019/01/21/687128474/analysis-how-the-rise-of-the-far-right-threatens-democracy-worldwide/

Golder, M. (2016). Far right parties in Europe. *Annual Review of Political Science*, *19*, 477–497.

Jefferson, T. (2011). *Jefferson writings* (M. Peterson, Ed.). New York: Penguin Group.

Koch, A. (1964). *The philosophy of Thomas Jefferson* (2nd ed.). Chicago, IL: Quadrangle Books.

Kossis, L. (2012). Examining the conflict between municipal receivership and local autonomy. *Virginia Law Review*, *98*(5), 1109–1148.

Mann, T. E., & Ornstein, N. J. (2016). *It's even worse than it looks: How the American constitutional system collided with the new politics of extremism* (2nd ed.). New York: Basic Books.

Matthews, R. (1986). *The radical politics of Thomas Jefferson: A revisionist view* (2nd ed.). Lawrence, KS: University Press of Kansas.

Norris, P. & Inglehart, R. (2019). *Cultural backlash: Trump, Brexit, and authoritarian populism*. New York: Cambridge University Press.

136   *Conclusion*

Sen, A. (2001). *Development as freedom*. Great Britain: Oxford University Press.

Talpin, J. (2011). *Schools of democracy*. Colchester, UK: European Consortium for Political Research.

Thoreau, H. D. (1996). *Thoreau political writings*, N. L. Rosenblum (Ed.). Cambridge: Cambridge University Press.

United States Senate. (1987). S. CON. RES. 76. In J. Barreiro (Ed.), *Indian roots of American democracy* (pp. 74–75). USA: Northeast Indian Quarterly.

Whitman, W. (1982). *Whitman: Poetry and prose*. New York: The Library of America.

Appendix

Participant Questionnaire

Public happiness is the joy one experiences from actively participating in local government in order to help that local governments function well.

1. How often do you feel public happiness from your work at PBNYC?

2. How often has your experience with PBNYC given you a better understanding of others involved with PBNYC?

3. How often does your experience with PBNYC give you a sense of belonging?

4. How often does your experience with PBNYC cause you to reflect on social justice (human rights & equality) issues?

5. If the previous answer is not never, how often has your position changed on social justice (human rights & equality) issues?

All five questions will have the following options for answers

o Never
o Sometimes
o About half of the time
o Most of the time
o Always

Index

Abdullah, C. 55, 64–65
Ackelsberg, M. 109
administrative hierarchy reorganization 2–3, 4–5, 46, 54
aggregate reasoning of political society 19–20
American Indians: influence on Jefferson 74–75, 116, 130; League of the Iroquois 9, 27, 41–42, 114–116, 130
American Renaissance 93
"The American Scholar" (Emerson) 95
apathy, political 21, 106–107, 118
Appadurai, A. 56
Arendt, H. 76, 77, 78, 79
Arrow, K. J. 121, 122
Ausserladschelder, V. 11
authoritarianism, far right populist 10–16, 128, 131, 134

Baiocchi, G. 4, 5–6, 20, 53, 55–56, 123–125
Bandura, A. 93–94
Barber, M. 87, 88, 90
Barrett, S. M. 74–75
Belo Horizonte, Brazil 50
belonging *see* sense of belonging
Bernhard, M. 10
Bhandari, H. 120, 121
Blee, K. 11, 12
Bloom, P. 70
Bolsonaro, Jair 10
bonding social capital 123
Bookchin, M. 74
Bortis, H. 26
Bosman, J. 23
Bourdieu, Pierre 120, 121
Bowling Alone (Putnam) 120
Brazil 18; Belo Horizonte 50; far right populist authoritarianism 10; Porto Alegre 4–5, 6–7, 27, 50, 55–56, 123–125; social justice 27, 50

Brexit referendum 14–15
bridging social capital 123
Brown, John 99
bureaucracies, corporate 83–84
bureaucracy, Mills' definition of 83–84
bureaucratic hierarchy reorganization 2–3, 4–5, 46, 54, 66
Bush, P. 35
"By Blue Ontario's Shore" (Whitman) 100

Cabell, Joseph 74
capital debate controversy of social capital 121–122
Causes of World War Three, The (Mills) 85, 105
CDP *see* Community Development Project (CDP)
ceremonial behavior 33, 34
ceremonial-instrumental dichotomy 33, 34
Chicago 18–19, 60
civic groups 3, 7, 46–47, 66, 67, 124–125, 132
civil rights *see* human rights
civil rights movement 106, 108–109, 110, 123
civil society, deliberative reasoning of 19–20
Coleman, James 120, 121
communicative dimension 3, 4, 47; implementation of recommendations 65–66; PBNYC case study 61–62, 65–66; recommendations 7–10, 61–65, 132; Talpin's study 56–60, 62–64; working groups 57, 59, 64–65, 68–69
Community Development Project (CDP) 48, 51, 61
community morality *see* morality
Concurrent Resolution 76, 116
Condolence Ceremony 115
Conkin, P. 41

conscience 96–99
consciousness-raising 108–110, 111, 125
consensus 4, 8, 41–42, 55, 66, 75, 94, 116, 130
corporate bureaucracies 83–84
Creasap, K. 11, 12
"Creative Democracy – The Task Before Us" (Dewey) 43, 104
cultural backlash 11–12
Cultural Revolution 12, 15, 133–134
cultural values 11, 12, 13, 15, 56

death, Whitman on 100–101
Declaration of Independence 42, 77, 116, 130
dehumanization 93–94
Del Valle Ruiz, Á. 129
deliberation *see* public deliberation
deliberative democracy 14, 22, 57, 63, 66
deliberative reasoning of civil society 19–20
Deliberative Transformative Moments (DTM) 65, 68–69
democracy: deliberative 14, 22, 57, 63, 66; Dewey on 43, 103–105, 127; erosion of quality of 128–129; far right populist threats to 10–16, 128; Foster on 34–35, 36; ideal of 1, 3, 7, 36, 39, 40, 57, 103–104, 108, 130, 134; managerialism and 22–23; participatory 3, 106–111, 133–134; pluralist 20–21; three types of decision-making 8; Whitman on 42–43, 100, 102–103, 131; *see also* local direct democracy
democratic society 42–43, 86, 105
"Democratic Vistas" (Whitman) 42, 100, 101–103, 131
Development as Freedom (Sen) 127–128
Dewey, John 16–17, 26, 39–40, 47, 73–74, 131; on democracy 43, 103–105, 127; influence on Port Huron Statement 107–108; on morality 103–105; scientific method 30–32; on understanding of others 81–82, 132
direct action 27, 46, 53, 66, 67, 108, 133
disagreement in public deliberation 59, 57, 64
discrimination 87–88, 90, 123, 128, 134
discussions, open-ended 53, 54–56, 66–67
diversity 13–14
"Divinity School Address" (Emerson) 95, 96
downgrading of democracies 128–129
Drolet, J. 12, 15
Dryzek, J. 9, 17, 21

DTM *see* Deliberative Transformative Moments (DTM)
Duterte, Rodrigo 10

economic insecurity hypothesis 11
Embree, L. 89–90
emergency manager laws 23
Emerson, Ralph Waldo 40–41, 93, 94–96
emotional hypothesis 118–119
equality: equity and 57; Schutz on 88–91; Whitman on 99–100, 103; *see also* inequality
"Equality and the Meaning Structure of the Social World" (Schutz) 87–88
equality of opportunity 57, 94; barriers to 88–91
equity 48–49, 57, 60–61, 62
ethical 26, 29, 34, 40, 87, 90, 103, 131
European Union 14–15
experts 3, 4, 6, 8, 14, 20, 22–23, 54, 64, 124, 131

face-to-face communication 38, 51, 61–62, 108, 131, 132, 133, 134; Dewey 47, 82; Mills 85, 117; Schutz 90; Talpin 119
facilitators 4, 21, 47, 55, 57; style 59; training 48, 61, 62, 63–64
far right populist authoritarianism 10–16, 128, 131, 134
Five Tribes *see* League of the Iroquois
Flacks, Richard 106, 107–108
Flint, Michigan 23, 128
Foa, R. 12, 13
Foster, John Fagg 33–37, 132
Frank, T. 12
Fugitive Slave Law (1850) 98
funding 3, 5, 46, 60, 65–66

Ganuza, E. 4, 5–6, 20, 53
Garrison, J. 82
Gilman, H. 48
Gingrich, Newt 128–129
global governance institutions 15
Gogoi, P. 10
Golder, M. 10, 11, 12, 13, 14, 15–16
grammar of public assemblies 62–63, 118–119
Great Law of Peace 115
Greenberg, E. S. 21
Grinde, D. 115, 116
group size 57, 59, 68

habits of thinking 16–17, 30, 86, 97
happiness, public 1, 3, 27, 70, 73–79, 116, 130–131

140 *Index*

Hartz-Karp, J. 123
Haudenosaunee *see* League of the Iroquois
Hayden, Tom 106–107, 108–109, 110
Hayduk, R. 49
Heller, P. 8–9, 20
His Journals (Emerson) 95
Hobolt, S. 14
human rights 8, 14, 48, 99–100, 109, 134;
    far right populist authoritarianism and
    10, 11, 15–16, 128

"I Sing the Body Electric" (Whitman) 100
idea-ranking tools 50–51
ideal of democracy 1, 3, 7, 36, 39, 40, 57,
    103–104, 108, 130, 134
Ikeda, D. 41, 81, 94, 95
immigration rights *see* human rights
individual morality *see* morality
individual preferences 19–20
individualism, society and 100, 101, 131
inequality 9, 11, 15–16, 20
Inglehart, R. 10, 13, 15
institutional adjustment theory 2, 33,
    35–37, 132
Institutional Economics 2, 26, 29–39
institution-technology dichotomy 30, 33
instrumental behavior 33, 34
instrumental primacy 36
instrumental theory of value 2, 33, 34–35
intangible benefits 1, 36, 70, 132; public
    happiness 1, 3, 27, 70, 73–79, 116,
    130–131; *see also* morality; sense of
    belonging; understanding of others
interdisciplinary research 27
intolerance 82, 94
Iroquois Confederacy 9, 27, 41–42,
    114–116, 130

Jabola-Carolus, I. 47, 51–52, 53, 54
Jaramillo, M. 68–69
Jefferson, Thomas 73, 74–79, 107, 116, 130
Johansen, B. 114–115, 116
Journal of Public Deliberation 123

Karpowitz, C. 55
Kateb, G. 99
Katznelson, I. 19
Koch, A. 77
Kossis, L. 23

LGBT rights *see* human rights
Lasswell 88
leaders: far right populist authoritarian
    10–16, 128, 131, 134; public
    deliberation and 59

League of the Iroquois 9, 27, 41–42,
    114–116, 130
Leaves of Grass (Whitman) 100
Lee, F. 28–29
Lerner, J. 48–49, 60
Levitan, L. 70
Lichtenstein, P. 29
Lincoln, Abraham 101
local direct democracy 1, 3, 29, 43,
    129–131; Jefferson's ward system 73,
    74–79, 116, 130; Thoreau on 41–42, 94

machine process 30
McIntyre, C. 96
Madison, James 79
Making Democracy Work (Putnam) 120,
    121
"Making Music Together" (Schutz) 88
managerialism 22–23
Mann, T. E. 128–129
Mansbridge, Jane 8
Marquetti, A. 6–7
mass media 84–85, 105–106, 117
mass society 85, 100, 103
Matthews, R. 75–76
means-end-continuum 32
meaning, finding 28; Dewey 39, 40, 81, 103;
    Mills 84, 85, 86; Port Huron Statement
    110; Schutz 86–88; Talpin 133
measurement 67–70
Mills, C. Wright: definition of bureaucracy
    83–84; influence on Port Huron
    Statement 107; on morality 105–106; on
    public deliberation 85–86, 106, 111; on
    sense of belonging 116–118, 133; on
    understanding of others 82–86, 132
Milner, H. 19
minimal dislocation 37
moral insensibility 105
morality 1, 93–111, 133–134; Dewey on
    103–105; Emerson on 94–96;
    measurement 70; Mills on 105–106;
    Port Huron Statement 106–111, 133;
    Thoreau on 96–99; Whitman on 99–103
Morris, D. 39, 40, 103
Morsang-sur-Orge, France 59, 63, 118
Moscrop, D. 57
Mounk, Y. 12, 13
multiculturalism 15, 128

Natanson, M. 86
"Nature" (Emerson) 94
New England townships 74
New York City *see* PBNYC (participatory
    budgeting in New York City) case study

Index 141

non-violent direct action 27, 46, 53, 66, 67, 108, 133
Norris, P. 10, 13, 15
Nussbaum, M. C. 100–101

O'Neill, D. 10
open-ended discussions 53, 54–56, 66–67
Ornstein, N. J. 128–129

participatory budgeting: concepts 17–20; objections to 20–22
Participatory Budgeting Project (PBP) 5, 48–49, 50–51
participatory democracy 3, 106–111, 133–134
Pateman, C. 63
PBNYC (participatory budgeting in New York City) case study 27, 37–38, 47–53, 132, 133; communicative dimension 61–62, 65–66; equity goals 48–49, 62; funding 46, 60, 65–66; implementation of recommendations 65–67; interface with city agencies 51–53; political dimension 46–47, 66–67; social justice method 50–51; training needed 48
PBP *see* Participatory Budgeting Project (PBP)
Phenomenology of the Social World, The (Schutz) 87
Philippines 10
philosophical research 3, 39–43
Piven, F. 109, 110
"A Plea for Captain John Brown" (Thoreau) 98–99
pluralism 14, 20–21
Poder, T. 120
political apathy 21, 106–107, 118
political dimension 2–3, 46–47; bureaucratic hierarchy reorganization 2–3, 4–5, 46, 54, 66; implementation of recommendations 66–67; open-ended discussions 53, 54–56, 66–67; PBNYC case study 46–47, 66–67; recommendations 3, 4–7, 53–56, 132, 133; sovereignty dimension 5, 53
Political Economy 26
political parties 4–5, 53–54, 59, 76, 77, 78, 128–130, 131
populism *see* far right populist authoritarianism
Port Huron Statement 3, 106–111, 125, 133
Porto Alegre, Brazil 4–5, 6–7, 27, 50, 55–56, 123–125
Power, M. 28

Power Elite, The (Mills) 85
practices of participatory budgeting 31–32
problem statement 31
procedures: participatory budgeting 31–32; public deliberation 57–59
project evaluation matrix 51
PT party, Brazil 4–5
public deliberation 3, 19–20, 21, 47, 133; conditions needed for 56–61; disagreement 59; equality of opportunity and 88–91, 94; equity 57, 60–61, 62; group size 57, 59, 68; implementation of recommendations 65–66; intolerance and 82, 94; leaders 59; League of the Iroquois 115–116, 130; measuring quality of 67–70; Mills on 85–86, 106, 111; morality and 93–94, 111; PBNYC case study 61–62, 65–66; procedures 57–59; recommendations 7–10, 61–65; self-reflection and 17, 93; stakes 60; story-telling in 68; Talpin's study 56–60, 62–64; working groups 57, 59, 64–65, 68–69
public happiness 1, 3, 27, 70, 73–79, 116, 130–131
public speaking training 62
publicity hypothesis 118–119
publics 85–86, 106, 111
"pursuit of happiness" 77, 116, 130
Putnam, Robert: on public happiness 73; on social capital 18, 119, 120, 121, 122, 123, 133

Quality of Life Index 50

Ranson, B. 33, 34, 35
Rao, V. 8–9
Raphael, C. 55
recognized interdependence 36–37
reconciliation between individualism and society 100–101, 103, 131
redistributive aspect of participatory budgeting 6–7
referendums 14
religion 12–13
Representative Men (Emerson) 40–41
Republican party 128–129
"Resistance to Civil Government" (Thoreau) 97–98
Roane, Spencer 76
Robison, L. 122
Rome Municipo XI, Italy 58, 59, 118
rules of participatory budgeting 31–32

Schutz, Alfred 86–91, 132

142 *Index*

scientific curiosity 30
scientific method 30–32
SDS *see* Students for a Democratic Society (SDS)
Secondo, D. 48–49, 60
self-reflection 17, 93, 95–96, 134
"Self-Reliance" (Emerson) 94
Sen, A. 8, 9, 127–128
Senate of the United States 116
sense of belonging 1, 114–125, 133; League of the Iroquois 114–116; Mills on 116–118, 133; social capital and 119–125; Talpin on 118–119, 133
Seville, Spain 59, 118
Shanley, M. 109
Shapiro, I. 39, 40, 103
Sigler, J. A. 82–83
Sintomer, Y. 17–18
Sitton, J. 76
Skidmore, M. J. 22, 93, 94, 95, 96
slavery 98–99
"Slavery in Massachusetts" (Thoreau) 98–99
SNCC *see* Student Nonviolent Coordinating Committee (SNCC)
social capital 18, 55–56, 61–62, 66, 119–125; bonding and bridging 123; capital debate controversy 121–122; history of 120–121; Putnam on 18, 119, 121, 122, 123, 133
social justice 5–6, 27, 50–51, 60–61, 106, 107
social movements 3, 12, 108–111, 133
social networks 18, 120, 121
social philosophers 3, 28, 39–43
social provisioning 1, 28–29, 35–36
Sociological Imagination, The (Mills) 83, 84, 86
"Song of Myself" (Whitman) 99–100, 101
"A Song of the Rolling Earth" (Whitman) 101
sovereignty dimension 5, 53
stakes, public deliberation and 60
Steiner, J. 67, 68–69
story-telling 68
Student Nonviolent Coordinating Committee (SNCC) 108
Students for a Democratic Society (SDS) 3, 27, 106–109
Sturgeon, M. J. 33, 36, 37
Su, C. 37–38, 48, 56
supranational institutions 15

Talpin, Julien 56–60, 62–64, 118–119, 133
technology 30, 33
Thompson, D. 66
Thoreau, Henry David 40, 93, 134; influence on Port Huron Statement 107; on local direct democracy 41–42, 94; on morality 96–99
Tilman, R. 30, 105
Tool, M. 33–35, 36, 39
training 3, 48, 61, 62–64, 132
Transcendentalists 17, 40–43, 93; *see also* Emerson, Ralph Waldo; Thoreau, Henry David; Whitman, Walt
Trump, Donald 10–11
turn-taking 57–58

understanding of others 1, 81–91, 132; Dewey on 81–82, 132; Mills on 82–86, 132; Schutz on 86–91, 132
United Kingdom 14–15
United Nations Habitat II meeting 4, 27

value aspect of participatory budgeting 5–6
Veblen, Thorstein 29–30

Walden (Thoreau) 97
Waller, W. 33
Walsh, G. (1967) 86–87
Wampler, B. 50, 60, 123
ward system 73, 74–79, 116, 130
Warren, M. 57
Weber, Max 86, 87
"The Well-Informed Citizen" (Schutz) 88
West, C. 95
Westbrook, R. B. 108
"When Lilacs Last in the Door Yard Bloom'd" (Whitman) 100
Whitman, Walt 13, 40, 93; on democracy 42–43, 100, 102–103, 131; on morality 99–103; on public happiness 73
Williams, M. 12, 15, 19
wisdom, love of 39–40
women's liberation movement 109–110
women's rights 99–100, 109; *see also* human rights
Worker's party *see* PT party, Brazil
working groups 57, 59, 64–65, 68–69

Yasunobu, K. 120, 121

Printed in the United States
by Baker & Taylor Publisher Services